*The Strength of the Hills*

George Ewart Evans

# *The Strength of the Hills*

## AN AUTOBIOGRAPHY

Illustrated by David Gentleman

*faber and faber*
LONDON · BOSTON

First published in 1983
This edition first published in 1985
by Faber and Faber Limited
3 Queen Square London WC1N 3AU

Printed in Great Britain by
Whitstable Litho Limited, Whitstable, Kent.
All rights reserved

*British Library Cataloguing in Publication Data*

Evans, George Ewart
The strength of the hills.
1. Evans, George Ewart   2. Historians——
Great Britain——Biography
I. Title
941′0072024    DA3.E9
ISBN 0-571-13550-1

I'm Rhieni

# Contents

penywaun

# 1 · The Valley

I was born in the mining village of Abercynon in Glamorgan on 1 April 1909. On many official occasions since I have been given a quizzical look from someone on the other side of a desk, and sometimes the date has even evoked a comment. A kindly old man was one of the first to remark on it. He was examining my fitness for entry into the grammar school, and gave me a professional, scholastic glare over his pince-nez: 'Were you born before twelve noon on the first of April?' 'At six-thirty in the morning, sir.' He took off his pince-nez and put his pen down. 'Well,' he said 'that really lets you out, doesn't it?'

Now I could see that he was joking and grinned as he said: 'Don't you worry, boy: I'll be surprised if you don't get through.' Looking back, I wish I'd been sharp enough to reply: 'Yes, sir, born before noon on the first of April, so I suppose I am a real April Fool.' But it's an advantage to be born on that day because I knew from the very beginning what it takes no end of people a lifetime to find out.

I am not one of those who have any cot or cradle memories, and as far as I know, I was never kissed in my perambulator. I doubt in fact that I was ever taken about in one, for my mother was too preoccupied in bringing up the rest of the family to spare time for parading any one of them. Yet I recall being visited at home once by my first teacher—the 'babies' teacher in the Infants' School. My mother brought her up to my bedroom but I heard her voice as she was coming up the stairs and pretended to be asleep to escape the embarrassment of her perfunctory kiss: I had probably already caused her enough trouble to preclude any real affection, and interpreted it as a mere parade of parent-teacher goodwill. Such early cynicism may well have been a precocious strain in my character.

A few days after my birth, I was later told, I very nearly escaped having to present myself to the outside world. Late one night I developed a noisy and distressing attack of croup; my gasping and croaking alarmed my parents and my mother sent for a neighbour who lived opposite. Mrs Ellis was a large, comfortable woman who had a fund of old traditional remedies. She immediately prescribed a teaspoonful of paraffin oil. They probably got it from a stable lamp, but anyway it served its purpose. In later years I often looked at Mrs Ellis as 'the good lady who saved your life'. The doctor, as it happened, was rarely seen in our house and there was a rather risky reliance on old wives' medicine. But none of us appeared to suffer for it, except on one occasion when Mother nearly left it too late to call in the doctor. One of my younger brothers had been ill with a high fever and a cough and the doctor came to identify it. He was just in time to inoculate him against a bad attack of diphtheria.

By modern standards we were a large family, but at that period large families were not unusual. In our corner of the village (or, more properly, little town of about 10,000 people) there were three tradesmen's families, each of which had reached double figures. People used to say that the Evanses, the Davieses and the Williamses were vying with each other to see who could produce the biggest brood. I believe the Evanses won. But my father had an advantage in that he was married twice.

Eventually he fathered a family that had almost Job's distribution— seven sons but four instead of three daughters. In his middle years especially, he must have acquired the patience of Job for then he had shoals of troubles as well as children to molest him. But he kept his health and his balance and lived for seven years beyond his allotted span.

I find it difficult to assess why my parents brought up such a large family: perhaps they did so because large families were in the fashion. Certainly any motive of providing for their own old age did not seem to fit their temperaments. When I was quite young I can remember more than one visitor coming to our household, looking round a full table and saying to my parents, 'What a large family you have! But there! Look how safe you'll be when you get old. They'll all be able to pay you back.' The obligation to care for your parents in their old age was accepted by my generation in Wales and the attitude implied in the phrase 'Pay them back' was the keystone of family solidarity.

My father, William Evans, moved up from Cardiff shortly after the coal-pit had been sunk at Abercynon in 1886. He had been apprenticed to a village grocer and later went on to Cardiff. When he had served his time he moved up to the valleys to start a business of his own. He had been born at Pentyrch, a village in the ancient borough of Llantrisant where his people had been hereditary freemen for generations. He started work at a very young age in the Powell Dyffryn colliery. His job was that of brattice-boy, usually about eight or ten years of age, whose task involved opening and closing the brattice, the wooden, canvas-covered ventilation door, that let through the haulier with his pony and 'dram' or tub of coal to and fro from coal face to pit bottom. It was a lonely job for a young boy with only a lighted candle and the brief company of the approaching haulier. Yet for my father it could not have been much more than a temporary job as a crippled right foot made actual mining impossible for him. Therefore his leaving the mine was inevitable, and he became apprentice to a grocer.

I had a vivid reminder of this period of his life when I was a small boy myself. At that time I was sleeping in my father's bedroom. In the corner of the room was a heavy steel safe where he kept his deeds and his valuables. Alongside the safe was a chest of drawers and in the second drawer from the top was a policeman's truncheon (I knew its position well as I was always opening the drawer to handle it). One day I asked him why he kept the truncheon in his bedroom. All was clear when he told me that once in Pentyrch when he was a youth and had been round the farms and cottages collecting accounts, he had been set upon and robbed of his master's money.

He often allowed me to look in his safe where he had a collection of coins, chiefly those that were just being withdrawn, as the currency saw a great deal of changes at the beginning of the First World War. There was a wash-leather bag, half full of gold sovereigns and half-sovereigns, the coins that had just been withdrawn from circulation. There were silver crowns (five-shilling pieces) and four-shilling pieces that I could vaguely remember being in use, and lastly a groat or fourpenny piece that had gone out well before my time. It reminded my father of an old lady in Pentyrch. Every week-end she used to hand her son a groat out of the wages he had given her, with the invariable warning formula: '*Dyma grot i ti, a phaid â meddwi*' (Here's a groat for you, and don't get drunk).

I remembered the shining, varnished truncheon many times in later years and it became a symbol of the illusory security given by all possessions. Although it may well have put my father's mind at ease, he found, not many years later, that there were even more painful and disastrous ways of losing money than through direct physical assault.

My father's first wife, Mary Edwards, bore him three children. She also came from an old Glamorgan family. She was niece to the younger James who composed the music to his father's words *Mae Hen Wlad Fy Nhadau*, the Welsh national anthem. This family claimed a link with the Stradlings, a family of Norman descent who built St Donat's Castle on the coast of Glamorgan, an ancient building that was bought by Hearst, 'Citizen Kane', the American newspaper magnate. St Donat's is now the site of Atlantic College, an international educational centre.

The James family, originally of Pontypridd, have a story that one of the Stradlings was hanged. It is not quite clear what his crime was, but legend has it that he was hanged either for sheep-stealing, or for ship-wrecking on the Tusker Rock, a treacherous reef just below the surface of the Bristol Channel. The story in the James family relates that physical evidence of the nefarious Stradling practice still remains in the actual physical make-up of his descendants. It is said that the original, forcible displacement of the victim's skull had caused the baso-occipital bone at the back of the head—where the spine joins the skull—to stand out prominently in all his descendants. I heard this legend in recent years from my eldest sister Gwladys and was very amused when I heard it for the man must have been well dead before he could transmit any pattern at all. But a few days after first hearing this story, a clear picture of the head of my eldest brother, Jack, came back in surprising detail and definition. About the end of 1917 he had been called up into the Royal Flying Corps, precursor of the R.A.F. In those days, the unit barbers gave all recruits a roundhead's haircut. On his first leave from Blandford Camp in Dorset he arrived home with the back and sides of his head shaved even closer to the skin than the modern crewcut. As I examined him carefully, I saw the memorable bone standing out like a half-formed carbuncle high up on the back of his neck. This physical mark of the family was a reality even if the account of its origin was pure fantasy.

There is another story in the family tradition that has a stronger claim to be true. It concerns the genesis of *Mae Hen Wlad Fy Nhadau*. James James, the composer of the tune, was improvising on the piano. His father, Evan, heard him and called out 'What's that tune you're playing? I like it! I like it! Get it down and I'll write some words for it.' This story came from Gilbert Harries, a retired clergyman, a nephew of my father's first wife. He passed on the story to me just before his death in Lowestoft in 1977.

In dredging up other early memories, I am reminded of the theory of Adler, one of the modern psychiatrists. He suggested that a man's earliest memories give a clue to his temperament and so, by implication, to the course of his later life. If this is so, some of my earliest memories heralded a life full of gloom and disaster, or at best, a consuming interest in the spectacular, even the morbid. One memory is very clear: that of the biggest disaster in British mining history. It happened in 1913 at Senghenydd in mid-Glamorgan, a mining village just over the hill and the moorland a few miles from my home. I recall clearly the photograph of the pit-head that appeared in the newspaper next day; but the impression etched indelibly into my four–year–old mind was the sight I beheld on the Sunday following. Our house backed on to Cefn Leyshon, part of the ridge of Mynydd Eglwysilian that separated us from Senghenydd. Hundreds of miners from the western valleys were walking over the hill to the stricken village. They wore their Sunday black and were climbing along the path over the hill, girding it as if with an emblematic mourning ribbon.

Llewellyn Jenkins, a boyhood friend, also remembers the disaster and describes it more graphically. 'I have the most vivid memories of the explosion, and recall sitting in the classroom at Abertaf and wondering, on going home, why there was a procession and crowds along the canal bank from Mountain Ash. It seemed as if there was a plague of flies crawling up the mountainside to get at the disaster.' The image stayed with me for years, and it was later reinforced when I met a man from the village of Senghenydd. He told me that all the men in the pit had been killed. The blast from the explosion was so massive that it blew the head off the banksman, the worker whose post was at the top of the pit shaft and who received the cage as it was wound up to the daylight. The complete death toll was 439.

Yet another disaster happened a fortnight later on 27 October. A tornado swept up the valley and wrecked a row of houses called 'Fair View'. The houses stood on an eminence half out of the valley and faced south, as distinct from the other streets that followed the valley's contours. The tornado was said to have begun near Exeter; it tracked north through Somerset and swept over the Bristol Channel, crossing the Welsh coast near Aberthaw. On its progress up the Taf valley it struck Cilfynydd and picked up a man who was walking in one of the streets and deposited him 400 yards away in a field. In Abercynon thirteen houses in 'Fair View' had their roofs blown off and their upstairs walls shattered. Two of the houses were completely wrecked and remained in ruins for most of the following war. Strangely enough the Cilfynydd man was the only fatal casualty. My memory of the tornado is vague although I must have heard the noise. I can remember the storm of rain that followed and I recall vividly standing on the doorstep of the shop, watching the water pouring down the street and wondering whether or not it would reach the toes of my boots which I had purposely stuck out beyond the step of the door.

Another early incident stands out very clearly. I am standing at the door of the middle room of the house: it is covered by a velvet curtain fixed to a brass rod. My mother is seeing a visitor to the front door. As they pause to open the curtained door, I feel very small beside them. But just as the door is being opened, I am struck with a sudden breathlessness. It is just as if two iron hands have clamped my chest in an unyielding grip. I am frightened and grip my mother's skirt gasping, 'Am I going to die? Am I going to die?' The two women are amused. My mother laughs and says, 'Go on with you, boy! There's nothing wrong with _you_.' This incident lay buried in my mind until early adolescence when this same breathing difficulty recurred inexplicably. It was in the morning assembly at the county school, held in the gymnasium, with everyone standing. The headmaster announced one of my favourite hymns, _Hyfrydol_, a beautiful melody and easy to harmonize. But when it came to the singing, I had no breath to sing a note. I stood dumb.

I was puzzled but not alarmed and told no one about this difficulty in breathing. This was a mistake but at that age I was steeped in the nonconformist ethic that urged you to be independent and take pride in making your own way, not even accepting help when it was offered. Later, at school, I was tackled by the headmaster for a bad reading of a psalm in school assembly. But I was too proud to tell him about the defect although he was not an unsympathetic man. Eventually, I did get over it myself, whatever it was. Perhaps I grew out of it or side-stepped it, instead of trying to meet it head on. How difficult I made it for myself, all because I was too independent to recognize that ultimately we _depend_ on one another and should accept and give help wherever there is need.

The First World War was the event that coloured the lives of all the people who were born in the first decade of this century. I remember vividly one isolated image from the day of its outbreak—a motor car going down the road to the next village, a newspaper placard fixed to its back with WAR DECLARED in big capitals. A car at that time was a rare sight in itself and although I couldn't grasp what was happening, I sensed from the reactions of the grown-ups that something very big was taking place.

My mother's youngest brother, George Hitchings, was a reservist in the Glamorgan Yeomanry; he was called up immediately, together with his mount, a Welsh cob. He lived in Maesteg, my mother's home, as did his brother Will: they bred Welsh cobs and George had taken one of these to the Boer War, about fifteen years before. In the early days of this new war, I was captivated by the glamour of the horse regiments. Even without his horse it was a sight to see a cavalryman marching down the street—with flared breeches, tightly rolled puttees, leather ammunition pouch, highly polished boots with spurs, and an idly swung swagger-stick. It was like watching our coloured lead soldiers coming to life and marching past admiring crowds. At that age we were mercifully unaware of the reality of war.

All our boyish fantasies became centred in the war, and as time went on it became a serious game to collect and wear the brass badges of your favourite regiment. Later, though, we began to feel the bite of the war, and it tore out a great deal of our fantasy. Tom Heck, the assistant in the shop, was called up and could not be replaced. He was always friendly and cheerful and I was sorry to see him go: I was sorrier still when I realized I myself was to be drawn into the relentless round of the business. But that came later.

Keeping a shop during the war was an arduous business. We opened at 9 a.m. and closed between 7 and 8 p.m. On Fridays and Saturdays businesses were open until midnight. From quite an early age I was expected to be somewhere around. One of my first jobs in the morning, when I was not at school, was to sweep out the customers' part of the shop. First I sprinkled the floor with water to prevent the dust from rising as I swept it. Then I got a hand bowl full of fresh sawdust from a sack in the little warehouse and sprinkled it on the clean boards. Next I had to run errands and to do various little jobs like drawing a pint of vinegar from a big barrel in the warehouse or sawing up blocks of salt with a special saw into a prescribed thickness, ready to be packed in brown paper. Later in the war, when sugar was very strictly rationed, we had a big barrel of molasses, a thick syrup, in the small warehouse. We could draw off a pint to fill a customer's empty jam jar.

Above the warehouse was the storeroom where there were shelves holding brightly coloured tin canisters decorated with Indian and

Chinese letters. Here was also a coffee machine in which we ground the beans when a customer wanted freshly ground coffee. In the storeroom was also the cheese rack. The Caerphilly cheeses were made in Penywaun farm which was only three or four miles from Caerphilly itself. Father bought the cheeses on a counter-account with Mrs Thomas: he took the cheeses she made and supplied her with the equivalent value of goods and animal foods. When the cheeses came from the farm they had been taken fresh from the moulds. They were placed in the wooden rack to mature and acquire a skin or rind. The round cheeses were about eight inches in diameter and about two inches thick. They stood on their ends in the inward sloping shelves for a fortnight or so when they came in during the spring or early summer.

I spent a great deal of time behind the counter, watching the stream of customers. When the gypsies came into the shop it was like a pageant. There were many of them travelling the road at that time. Two women usually 'worked' the valley, bringing with them two or three children and very often a baby in arms, 'Welsh fashion', expertly tucked in a shawl and held with one hand, so that the other was free to carry her basket of pegs. After they had hawked their wares round the village they came into the shop. They had made their pegs in a temporary encampment at the foot of the hill and it was important not to take any home. Their visit began with a kind of barter. They would try to sell my father the remnant of the pegs and then start to bargain with him for odd pieces of bacon, dry cheese or anything they could buy cheaply. When they had finished at the provision counter, Father would open a tin of broken biscuits and pack them up for the children. He treated the gypsies with an easy affability: he knew many of them well because they had been visiting the shop for years in their regular progress round the country.

We now had to endure the German U-boat campaign against our food supplies. The heavy physical work of the steelworkers and coalminers demanded more than the skimpy rations available. Cheese, I recall, was the commodity most in demand. One evening a crowd of people appeared outside our shop and two aggressive men came in and spoke to my father. They had heard that a consignment of cheese had been delivered to William Evans: 'When are you going to start selling it?'

Father denied that he had any cheese to spare: the two men could search his two warehouses if they doubted his word. My brother Jack chipped in and said, 'And you can search under my bed, if you like!' The crowd dispersed a few minutes later, convinced that no stock of cheese was being hoarded in this shop. But the threatening aspect of the crowd made a deep impression on me.

As the war progressed, life became increasingly difficult for my parents. My mother was small-boned with dark curly hair and blue eyes. She was wiry and volatile, very rarely ill, and lived to the age of ninety-five after a life that was exceptionally hard. When the shop was prospering she had plenty of domestic help, but later she had little assistance.

My most burdensome job was looking after Daisy the cow. After my eldest brother had been called up, I was effectively tied to Daisy's tail. I had to take her out most mornings to graze and then fetch her back. But that was far from the end of my involvement. When the fences of the Bottom Field fell into disrepair, Daisy charged out of the field looking for more succulent grazing. More than once she broke into the allotments and ate up the cabbages. Once I lost her for more than two hours until one of my schoolfellows told me: 'Your cow is at Jenkins Goitre Coed.' This farm was half a mile away, on the hill above the village. When I caught up with her I apologized to old Mr Jenkins the farmer. He looked understandingly at the old cow and said in his deep voice: 'No harm, *bach*. Bulling she is: bulling no doubt.' An incident that was another step in my education.

At last Daisy's wanderings came to a sad end. One day she broke through the fence and grazed for a long time on the lush growth down by the river. She got blown and had to be killed by the local butcher. I cannot remember my own feelings at the time but Mother was very upset. She was attached to Daisy and felt her death more than any of us.

I believe it was a Thursday when the war came to an end—the eleventh hour of the eleventh day of the eleventh month of 1918. As we sat in school that morning we suddenly heard the pit hooter sounding at an unusual time and continuing longer than usual. Peace at last. That evening a group of boys arranged a torchlight procession in our street. The end of the war was celebrated in our house by hanging candle lanterns round the front windows. A neighbour brought up a bottle of whisky and drank with Father to the new era that was just beginning.

Yet was the war over? The fighting had finished but we were to be sadly reminded of its lesser effects. The birchwood high above the River Taf had been cut down during the war years. In spring the floor of the wood had been carpeted with bluebells. Snipe had nested above the slope and we could often see kingfishers on the river banks. The war in fact saw the final denudation of the valleys. But the hills remained.

Walking on the hills I was a different being: I had left behind the tensions of the home and shop and there was a glimpse of new beginnings and an exciting promise of the future. Most of my early excursions were official journeys to the farms on the hills. I went with Father or my brother Jack at first, but later I took the horse and cart up myself. If I went with Jack, I got out of the cart at the steep climb out of the valley and walked up a grassy path to avoid the loop of the ascending road along which Jack led the horse and cart. Once we were on the fairly flat back of the hill, I clambered back into the cart and we were away past the farms, Y Llechwen, Y Garth Fawr, Y Garth Fach through winding lanes bordered by low stone walls. Farther beyond Llechwan was a farm kept by Mr Miles. On an early visit there, my father stopped to call on his old friend and he left my younger brother Roy and me in the trap. While he was inside one of the farmer's daughters brought out a couple of glasses of milk for us. Roy, who was about four and hadn't been used to drinking out of a glass, took a bite at his and broke a chunk out of it.

The visits to the hill farms were the highlights of our days and from an early age I peopled them in my imagination with a different class of being. There was a hollow, not far from the Miles farm, called Pant y Ddawns (The Hollow of the Dance) which fairies were supposed to frequent and were actually seen by some people. Another small farm was shown me as the place where the mother of a young baby had forgotten to place the poker over its cradle: as a consequence the child, unprotected by iron, had been stolen by the fairies and replaced by a 'changeling'. I was young enough to believe these tales implicitly, but my early sense of wonder in the hills has never entirely vanished.

We often visited Penywaun, a big farm near the highest point of the 'mountain', as we invariably called the hills when we were young. Mr Thomas Penywaun was one of my father's first customers at the shop and he became a firm friend. But he died rather young, leaving his widow to carry on the farm and bring up their three children. Mrs Thomas always made us welcome, whether we were delivering goods or taking a pleasure trip in the trap. As soon as we arrived after our long pull from the valley, she would arrange to have the horse taken out of the shafts. A farm worker who lived in the house would stable him and give him water and a handful of hay.

Mrs Thomas was the model of the traditional hospitality of the old hill community: whoever called it was a point of honour to welcome them. She was a very efficient, neat woman with a reddish face, her hair parted in the middle and drawn back tightly against her head. She rarely smiled but this was not through a lack of good nature: her responsibilities had given her a serious expression. As soon as she helped the maid to clear the table, we had our feet under it, after first washing our hands. The table was a very long one, with bare scrubbed boards; there were no chairs, only benches. There was always a full company of farm workers, maids and visitors. It was always a high-tea with toasted cheese, homemade bread and butter, and *bara brith* loaves that were sweetened by dried fruit, literally 'speckled bread'.

There were many visits like these; but what I have since marvelled at, having spent so much time in eastern England, is the difference there was between the two cultures. Mrs Thomas accepted our calling, and we—when she came down into the valley—accepted her calling unannounced. This was the traditional response to everyone, even a stranger: you welcomed him and broke bread with him or at least offered him a cup of tea. It was an offence against the clan mores to give even a stranger a cold welcome. This was built into the old Celtic culture. But it was quite different in the Cambridge area where I had my first job. If I was invited to a meal it was hedged in, as I soon found out, by a strict protocol. If you were asked out to tea you were expected to lose yourself by six o'clock; and I committed an English gaffe more than once, until my landlady hinted that I should depart at the recognized time. This was hard for me to realize coming straight from south Wales where the custom was that if you were invited out to tea you were expected to stay the whole evening. And it was not a matter of class, for I remember when I was at university my Latin master at school invited me to tea with his wife. After the meal I made a tentative move to leave, not being sure what was the proper thing to do. But his wife said I must stay to supper as it was already prepared. We went on talking and had a pleasant evening. That was the usual custom at home: you were asked out to tea and you spent the rest of the evening either in earnest discussion, or less usually in talking in a social way, or singing round a piano.

As an Englishman knows, not long after he has crossed the border, he is in a different country, so the Welshman crossing into England a half century ago was soon aware that he too was in a strange land. Even after living in England for about half a century I still have reminders of the difference of the two cultures. One example will perhaps show this. In recent years we bought a small cottage in East Anglia, and since the houses in the village were not numbered we had to choose a name. It was a very old cottage and had been almost derelict for eighteen years, and someone else in the meantime appropriated the name that was on our deeds. We called the cottage 'The Garth' out of nostalgia, as it was once a sixteenth-century farmhouse very much the same age as the farmhouse above my home that had the name 'Y Garth Fach'—The Little Garth. There was a bit of a joke in calling it by this name, too, a kind of *lucus a non lucendo* (it's called a *grove* because it doesn't shine); for the Welsh name for a garden is *gardd*, which is allied in meaning to the Middle English *garth*. That is the one thing our cottage did not have: at its back there was a wilderness. Shortly after we moved in an acquaintance called on us, and as she was leaving she looked at the cottage and said: 'Rather pretentious name for a small cottage, isn't it?' Then I realized that the name 'garth' had different undertones in England, and it looked as if our visitor had thought from the name that 'we fared to have gone up in the world', as they say in Suffolk, and were now living in a mansion; and she was a bit disappointed in our cottage.

So much for the unavoidable misunderstandings between the Welsh and the English. It is not that there is no snobbery in Wales but there are none of the inbuilt, stratified divisions that arise out of the hierarchical social structure of southern and eastern England. These divisions arise mainly out of the soil, as one of the main effects of a traditional arable culture, that lent itself later to a Norman, feudal overlay that persisted until very late. Wales, like the rest of the Celtic countries, as well as the north of England, had a pastoral economy. (Incidentally, I believe it to be the root difference, even between the north and the south of England.) Yet Wales was different in a particular sense in that after 1485 many of the *uchelwyr* (literally, 'the top men') followed Henry Tudor to London and the court leaving a decaying squirearchy and a poor peasantry who preserved their national identity mainly through Bishop Morgan's translation of the Bible into Welsh. This gave them as a people a new focus and fresh aspirations. This poor but vigorous peasantry, that reached from pre-medieval times right up to the first decades of this century, was still alive on the hill farms of Glamorgan. Although there had been improvements in farming and in stock-breeding in parts of Wales, many of the hill-farmers of Glamorgan were using the same tools and methods and had the same outlook as the hill-people of many centuries before. This was not evident to me when I was very young but it was in 1955 when I went back to my home to do a *Return Journey* feature for the B.B.C. and revisited some of the hill-farms.

One of the farms I remembered very well was Penygraig, kept by John

Evans and his sister. The mountain that partly overlooked the next village of Cilfynydd was called Craig Evan Leyshon and the farm was at its summit, hence its name 'Penygraig' (top of the rock or hill). On the side of the hill near our village the slope had been used to make a coal-tip where waste from the colliery was bucketed up on an endless rope and tipped. The hillside was all common land and Penygraig Farm had the sheepgrazing rights. They may also have been drawing the coal royalties, for at this period before nationalization the landowner drew royalties on every ton of coal drawn from the mine. In any case, the Evans family of Penygraig had the right to take all the coal on the tip that had slipped through the screening process at the surface of the pit. This coal was sold down in the valley and I recall that my father bought much of it on a counter-account. On one occasion I went with Jack taking goods to Penygraig. After climbing the steep hill we took the cart into the farmyard and carried the goods to the stone platform with a low stone wall at the back of the house—exactly like the platform at Penywaun. John Evans the farmer, a not very big man with grey hair, stood watching us from the other side of the yard, then he came forward and greeted us as we carried the goods to the door. Miss Evans, his sister, was inside and Jack took the goods into the house while I went back to the cart. I never penetrated into the farmhouse. In fact I was a bit afraid of Miss Evans on my first visit: she looked a bit like a wizened old witch. But she was friendly, and later brought out a glass of milk for me. It was her appearance that made her so odd: she was always dressed in black when she came down to the shop, with a black bonnet-type of hat, a long coat with lace at the front, a long black skirt and high button boots. Her dress was like the Queen's, though the old Queen had been dead about sixteen years since. She continued to wear the same outfit to the end of her life. John, her brother, died before her because I remember Jack telling me that he took his coffin up to the farm. James Howell the undertaker, who had his workshop the other side of the chapel, had persuaded Father to let Jack take the coffin, covered up with a sail cloth, up the hill. Jack told me that when he carried the coffin into the house the undertaker had asked him to help place old John in it. He said he had lifted up the feet, with his head turned away over his shoulder.

Old Miss Evans stayed on in the farm some time after her brother died. The last time I saw her at the farm she was in her working clothes: mob cap, a black blouse and skirt, with a grey flannel apron and heavy hobnailed boots. It was just before she gave us permission to cut some bracken off the common below the coal-tip. We used it as bedding for the animals. We did this on a Monday, on a bright half-term holiday from school: Jack scythed a strip of the bracken and I forked it up ready to cart it, while Dick the horse nibbled the grass between the hard stones. In spite of the dark, lowering coal-tip, the bright autumn sunshine was proof against its sinister gloom. It was in fact one of the 'dangerous' tips and a few years later it slipped without warning down the slope of the hill right across the common and on to the road. Fortunately, the black avalanche met nothing on its way, just missing the Powderhouse where they kept the dynamite that was used for blasting the rock underground. It was an ominous presage of what was to happen many years later at Aberfan, a few miles up the valley.

Yet I did not recognize the Evans family of Penygraig as some of the last members of the old immemorial community of the hills until I had talked with Edward Thomas of Penywaun. I had seen them with the eyes of a young boy, but Edward who knew them well was able to interpret them with the mind of a man. At Penywaun, years later, he told me about John Evans and his sister as they were at the first two decades of this century: I sensed as a boy they were unusual but now I recognized how different they were. John Evans the farmer did not buy a *gambo*, the traditional farm cart of Glamorgan, until 1902 or 1903. He paid £4.10s.0d. for a secondhand one at a sale. Previously the only vehicle he had was a *car llusg*—a slide–car, one of the most primitive vehicles used in animal traction. It had no wheels and the horse was harnessed to two long shafts that he dragged along the ground. The load was fixed across the poles of shafts by means of a wicker basket or a wooden container made to fit horizontally on the sloping shafts. The slide-car was as old as history yet it had one advantage: the farmer could carry loads on gradients where it would be dangerous to take a wheeled cart. Yet the contrast that presented itself to me as Edward Thomas described it was dramatic: down in the valley less than half a mile away was a modern colliery with all the latest gadgetry of modern technology, while the hill farmers (at least some of them) were still in the Middle Ages—even earlier, as far as their material culture was concerned. And how early was their pattern of living Edward Thomas revealed when he mentioned that John Evans still believed in fairies. So fixed was his belief that after he had shut in his cattle for the night nothing would induce him to come out after he had gone to bed. Even if a beast was ill, she had to get on with it herself until it was light and he went out to do the milking. I can give full credence to Edward Thomas's witness out of my own experience in Ireland and East Anglia: there are no retrospective limits to the evidence one can get of the age of the old community that lasted until the recent past. Take, for example, John Evans's fear of the fairies. One of the most attractive features of the Glamorgan hill landscape is the whitewashed farmhouses: *muriau gwynion Morganwg* (the white walls of Glamorgan) were celebrated in medieval Welsh poetry; and even today they can still be seen glinting in the spring sunshine. They fit the Glamorgan scene perfectly. But the people who built them are likely to have had other preoccupations besides natural beauty: one of these was the unseen life that went on around them—good and evil. It was against the evil influences that they had to take precautions; and white was one of their defences against them, their first assurance—as in other parts of the world—a sure bulwark to the place where they were to spend most of their days.

*farms near Abercynon*

Abercynon

## 2 · *The Shop*

Later when I was old enough to drive the cart I used to see a lot of Ivor Thomas, the baker. He had a shop in the same street. I called frequently at his place for one reason or another. He was an old widower who kept a shop where he sold his own bread. The shop was under the charge of his unmarried daughter, Bessie. Ma and Dinah, as we called my eldest sister, used to bake quantities of yeast-cake for sale in the shop, and that was the reason for my visits. I took the tins of cake in a huge square basket to the bakehouse, and often while we were waiting for the cakes to be done the old man used to tell me about the village. He was a companionable man with short, grey hair and a bristly moustache, and since baking was a lonely job he liked someone to talk to. He had been in the valley many years before my father, and liked to describe it before it was opened up by the colliery; especially the story of the ancient ford and the ruined bridge which was then the only bridge across the river. He gave an exact picture of the oldest part of the village called the Basin, whose cottages were still whitewashed in the old Glamorgan style. The Basin dated from the end of the eighteenth century when the Glamorgan canal was built to take the iron from the Cyfarthfa Ironworks at Merthyr Tudful down to the coast. Ivor Thomas first told me about the Cornishman, Richard Trevithick, who built the 'First Railway in the West' as a result of rivalry between two Merthyr ironmasters. At first Homfray the ironmaster built a tramway on stone sleepers; and four horses drew the loads of iron to the Basin where the iron was off-loaded on to the waiting barges. But the following year, 1804, for a wager Trevithick carried a load of ten tons of iron plus seventy passengers and Homfray won £1,000 off his fellow ironmaster Crawshay. The Basin was a kind of dock where there was a slight incline down which the iron was unloaded for its journey to Cardiff.

My last memory of Ivor Thomas was being taken by Bessie to his bedroom to await his orders. He had a very heavy cold and Father had lent me to him for the morning. He had run short of fuel for his oven, and I was to take the horse and cart to the nearest gasworks to get a load of coke. The old man was reclining in his bed like a doll, the sheet folded back in a spotlessly white roll, a shawl around his shoulders, and his hands outside so that he could more easily explain what he wanted me to do, where I was to go, and so on, and so on—at length. I was about thirteen and with all the confidence of that age considered I was above instruction having done the journey before with one of my brothers. But I received my orders as gracefully as I could; and I spent a pleasant morning getting the coke from Treharris gasworks and bringing it back to its place behind the bakehouse oven. Mr Thomas had a bristly terrier called Togo who was not too happy about my intrusion on his master's premises. One evening shortly after this, while the old man and his daughter were at chapel, someone doped the bristly Togo and ransacked the premises.

Following the brief jubilation at the end of the war there was almost an immediate change in the atmosphere. The influenza epidemic and the numerous deaths brought a fog of gloom into the valleys as it did to most built-up areas. But in 1920 there was a subtler change that I noticed but, naturally, could not interpret. My father was more inward looking: as I moved about the yard at the back of the shop I sometimes saw him staring out of the window over his desk; and he did not seem to see me as I made my way past the window and out down the side of the shop on to the road: previously he had always tapped the window to ask me where I was going. Only a few months before he had given me a ten shilling note—a fortune for a small boy at that time—as a reward for helping in the business: now I was getting very little. Then Hector, my second eldest brother who had left school, now left the shop and went to work with Howell Davies, Father's fellow-tradesman, a few yards down the street. He had launched out into a new business: besides baking bread and brewing beer he now invested in old army motor lorries that were sold off cheaply. I well remember a 'Napier', a very wide-bodied vehicle among the others. At first he used two or three of these to cart his beer about the valleys. Then he started up a charabanc business, something new at this time, advertising open coach rides to the coast or trips to the Wye Valley or mid-Wales. This was the start of the opening up of the valleys to private bus firms, usually begun by tradesmen such as Howell Davies; he himself started a prosperous bus service from the valleys to Cardiff and Swansea.

Almost immediately after the war there had been unrest. The governments failed to keep their promises to the soldiers returning from the front. The miners were pressing for better conditions, and the nationalization of the mines. The government set up a Royal Commission headed by Lord Justice Sankey. His report recommended that the present system of mine-ownership should be changed and that the colliery workers should have an effective voice in the direction of the mines. The government rejected nationalization and the miners were convinced that they had been bluffed.

My father must have been certain in his own mind that a strike was inevitable, and I have often wondered what his thoughts were about the coming conflict. He had weathered one strike before—in 1898 when the men were out for five months. Yet I never heard him say a word against the miners who were the bulk of his customers. Indeed, from his own experience he knew what the miners' life was like; in the 1898 strike he had given them credit, and the majority of them did not let him down when the strike was over. He was a liberal in politics, as most of Wales was at the end of the nineteenth century. William Ewart Gladstone was his hero: I was named after him, and Gladstone became one of my nicknames. He was held up as a kind of model of behaviour, and when I hurried over a meal to get out as soon as I could to whatever I was interested in, I was reminded that Gladstone had made a practice of chewing each mouthful of food thirty-two times—and look what a sterling figure he had become, able to chop down trees in his old age!

But although his political acumen had not progressed beyond personalities my father must have known out of experience and instinct what the conflict would result in. Our valley, like the Rhondda valleys, turned out the best steam-coal that was used almost solely by the Royal Navy. This showed in the names of the companies that owned the collieries and even in the names of the collieries themselves: the Maritime, the Ocean, Nixon's Navigation, the Deep Navigation and so on. But now coal had a rival: the first ocean-going ship burning oil was a Danish ship *Selandia*, launched in 1912, and the war hastened the use of oil in cargo ships. Already there was talk of changing over from coal-burning ships to oil; and if the present discontent continued and resulted in another strike, or lock-out, the steam-coal valleys would never recover from it. No wonder father looked grim and was tetchy with us children.

The conflict came to a head with the lock-out of 1921, the first overt symptom of a movement that began the break-up of the valley communities as they were at the beginning of the century. The year began with a lyrical spring. After a late fall of snow in our valley there was an explosion of growth and colour; the trees quickly put on their thick garments of leaves, the young grass flourished with an abundant growth earlier than usual. As I opened the gate to the cow, her steps quickened to get to the lushest patch of the pasture: the horse, as soon as I took the halter to him, kicked up his heels, skirted the field at full gallop, stopped suddenly and got on to his back and then rolled to and fro, his hoofs high in the air. He then struggled to his feet, shook his mane and began his steady enjoyment of cropping the young grass. The good weather lasted virtually until the autumn. Every day was full of sunlight and it hardly rained at all. At first plenty of water came down from the perpetual springs in the hills. With the lock-out and the closure of the collieries the water ran as clear as in pre-coal days; and by the summer trout began to return to the rivers, and even the otters. On one Sunday morning we had gone down to that part of the river where we swam during the week, (we weren't allowed to swim on Sunday; we had been to chapel and had our best clothes on), when we saw two men with a dead otter. One of them had seen it sporting in the pool, had slipped home to his house in Graig Berthlwyd and got a German Mauser revolver he had brought home from the Western Front and shot it.

One of the delights of the younger miners that summer was to dam some of the hill streams, making a pond large enough for them to swim in. There was hardly a day when they could not swim or sit in the sun. The older men worked on their allotments or sat in groups on the hillside, when they weren't organizing soup kitchens for the children and arranging concerts and amusements to help away the long hours of idleness. The weather was so outstanding one could almost believe that some well disposed Equalizer had attempted to balance the murk and gloom of the industrial scene with the saving grace of a six months' summer. For statistics show that it was the driest and sunniest summer that we are likely to meet in this century. It was not such a long stoppage as the later 1926 lock-out; but later in the year, exactly like the farm workers, the miners found their wages depressed in real terms below the

1914–18 level. After this, and especially the fiasco of the Sankey Commission, there could be no stability in the valleys and the communities they had nourished. The great diaspora from south Wales began at that time, a movement that resulted in half a million people leaving the region before the outbreak of the Second World War.

Tension at home now increased. The business had taken a bad blow. For the months of the lock-out, little money had been coming in though an amount of goods had been going out: only the schoolteachers, and a few small tradesmen or professional people were paying customers. It meant that the shop had to exist on the capital it had accumulated in easier times. Father, it appeared, had little fluid money. His capital was in property he had bought when business was flourishing. I knew about these houses for when I was younger I had gone with him on an occasional afternoon to collect the rent. These were three or four miners' cottages in the long terraces that lined the valley. I recall the visits very well. For writing in the rent books Father carried a silver inkwell and a metal pen which slid back into its case: these were the days before the fountain pen reached the valleys. I was fascinated by his carrying the inkwell in his pocket without the ink spilling. Father also owned the group of houses that included his shop and another shop farther up the street. He sold this to a tailor friend of his some years before. In the hope that things would 'pick up' as they had done after the 1898 strike, he began selling the terraced houses. The first he sold was to the Glamorgan County Council; and we soon had a policeman living next door to us. The business was thus kept going by an injection of money from the sale. But this money did not last long and another of the houses had soon to be sold. I came to divine when a house was being changed into money. Dinah, who was now responsible for the shop accounts, would be closeted with Father in the middle room for an evening, with only a brief visit from Ma who was now fully occupied with the family, having no maid now permanently living in. Later I had a suspicion that Ma strongly resented being excluded from the making of major decisions about the selling of houses, and though an effort was made by everyone to keep up the front of business-as-usual, this made the underlying tensions in the family more marked.

I sometimes wonder, as I look back, what my father was really like: how did he react to the bleak outlook? For at the time as a young boy I took the family for granted and did not pause in the hurly-burly of family life to consider each member as a person. By this time Father was fifty-six years old, and he spent the greater part of his time at home, concerned chiefly with the business. He liked congenial company, and had taken an active part in the affairs of the village as a member of the board of guardians, who were still operating shortly before that period. He belonged to a local tradesmen's association: was superintendent of the Sunday school and helped to organize the annual outing. For his relaxation he would often pack as many of the younger children as he could into the trap and take us down to his home in Pentyrch to visit members of his family—usually cousins—who still lived there; or he would go on to the hills to visit customers like the Thomases who were his friends. He occasionally visited London to stay with a sister who was married to an inspector in the Metropolitan Police. He told me of one occasion before I was born, when he went up with his brother David, who also had a business as a grocer and baker on the other side of the village. They were in a pub in Piccadilly, or maybe it was in Leicester Square, and were introduced to Jim Corbett, the world champion heavyweight boxer. What impressed them both was the size of the boxer's hands as he greeted them.

Father was essentially kind but it was not easy to judge his feelings. As a contrast to Ma, he rarely commented directly on people: and he kept his opinions to himself. He seemed easy-going, and I often thought that Ma had a better business sense than he had, and it was one of her frustrations that she was so tied with the children that she had virtually no hand in the running of the shop. Under the new pressure he seemed almost inert; but there was little he could do. A blight had fallen on the whole area and he continued to run the shop on his modest capital, hoping against all the odds that it would clear. Instead, it got worse. Father would sell a couple more houses and for a time things would look brighter. Then a threat came from another quarter. The local Co-operative Stores opened a branch in our street in a grocer's shop that had been empty for years. His business met the competition of a vigorous, collective store and immediately pressure began to be felt. It was obvious that the shop was going downhill. In the first place it was not well stocked, and the shelves were dressed up with a consignment of new soap and other packaged goods that were beginning to come on to the market with their family advertisements. No longer was I proud to stand near the shop as someone who was connected with a thriving business. But it was the remark of a classmate in the county school I had just entered that abruptly drew aside the veil. He had been engaged as an errand boy by a grocer at the other side of the village, and passing our shop one day he said to me: 'Not many people go to your shop now.'

Yet youth has a fund of resilience. Jack seemed cheerful and he relied on me to give him active help which I was happy to do as it meant help with responsibility. By the time I was twelve I was able to look after the horse and to take goods out in the cart. The only stress times were when I had been picked for one of the school teams that played on a Saturday morning—the busiest time of the week in the shop. But Jack would usually release me, taking on the extra work if the match was an important one. I was now in the county school a distance of four miles from home: we travelled by train, a new experience I welcomed because I was away all day and escaped midday chores that were likely to crop up when I was home. The school was bigger but not in such a pleasant position as Abertaf. It was housed in temporary buildings built about fourteen years before. They were corrugated iron with the classrooms cold in winter and often stiflingly hot in summer. The playgrounds were small platforms hewn out of a slope. There was no turf and we played football with a round ball since rugby was not possible. The rugby pitch was a half mile up the valley. The school environs were aggressively industrial: about a hundred yards from the classrooms was the headstock or winding-gear of the colliery. The winding engine was steam driven at that time, and lessons went on against a staccato sequence of rapid blasts, as the full cages of coal were wound up the pit. Then there was comparative silence as they went down.

Another eruption would cause a teacher who was in full flight either to screw up his face in annoyance or to pause in passive resignation. The railway line ran between the colliery and the school, and there was a more or less perpetual undercurrent of noise, of wagons being shunted or the trains to and from Cardiff whistling warnings of their approach. Yet both staff and pupils became inured to the industrial obbligato, and on the surface at least took little notice. Undoubtedly, the atmosphere took its toll in the extra strain on achieving concentration. But it was a friendly school with a staff that did wonders in such an unfavourable environment, turning out from the 'Old Tin Shanty', as it was called, a small crop of pupils that reached the top in medicine, law, religion, education and sport. Pupils of my years spent four years at the old site—before the school moved to its permanent home. The head-master, Watkin U. Williams, spent eighteen years in the 'temporary' buildings before he was able to take the school to Dyffryn House a mile or so away.

In 1924 I went with a number of boys from school to a Welsh Secondary Schoolboys' Camp in mid-Wales. Many of the boys came from the bigger schools in the coastal towns and we sensed that they were different from us. They were better dressed and better mannered than we were and had a much more confident, social deportment.

It was interesting to learn later that the pupils from schools like Cardiff High School realised that *they* too were different from us. Goronwy Rees, the writer, was at the 1924 camp the same time as the Mountain Ash 'brigade'. He was a Welsh nonconformist minister's son and has chronicled his reaction to meeting the boys from the mining valleys. His account is more sympathetic to someone who, at the time, had been drilled by circumstances and an occasional excursion out of the valley into the conviction that we came from a disadvantaged environment where the sun did not shine as brightly, literally and metaphorically, as elsewhere, and therefore could not expect to be looked upon as favoured plants. He wrote about twenty years ago:

I knew very little of the world outside the tiny frontiers of my birthplace [Aberystwyth] until at the age of thirteen I attended a camp organized for Welsh secondary schoolboys, and there made acquaintance for the first time of contemporaries, and their seniors, from the mining valleys of south Wales. To me they were like creatures of another race—bigger, rougher, tougher, uncouth and barbarian, jeering and foul-mouthed; I might have been an ancient Roman confronted for the first time by the Goths. But they also seemed freer and more adult and less inhibited than the boys I had known, scornful of authority, untouched by the miasma of bigotry and hypocrisy which emanated from the twenty-four chapels of our little town. Later when my father had moved to south Wales I came to know them better, played football against them, and in the years of mass unemployment saw these same boys and their fathers, lounging in their hundreds in the streets of some mining town, leaning against the lamp-posts smoking stubs of cigarettes, or racing their greyhounds against each other on the hill-tops above the valley; and even in the intolerable boredom and waste of unemployment they retained a kind of *farouche* independence which preserved their human dignity.

This was probably a just estimate of most of the boys who came from the valleys. It is certain we had little surface polish; and if we found ourselves in a situation where it was obvious that this lack had been noticed, rather than attempt to correct it we would out of contra-suggestion overemphasize it. Just as if we were to propose to ourselves:

'You've given us a bad name. Right, we'll live up to it.' Though nothing was said at the camp itself the 'Mountain Ash Gang' was referred to in the magazine report of the camp with hardly flattering implications.

It was, however, a memorable first holiday, full of the kind of scene to evoke during a night when sleep eludes the mind that is worried or has been too active, and cares and anxieties crowd headlong past the mind's eye. The imprint of the images stamped on my memory by that week in mid-Wales well over a half-century ago remain as sharp as ever: after a day of rain, the sun going down in a red haze, the Snowdon range black silhouettes to the north, Ynys Enlli floating like a dish in a calm sea, its edges turned up as though to keep themselves clear of the water, and the Braich y Pwll peninsula reaching out its long arm to take hold of the dish to see what sacred treasure trove it held. Then there was Cader Idris, the mountain we never did conquer. First we lost our way; then we had been put on the right path by an old shepherd and we were climbing purposefully only to get lost in the mist that came down suddenly when we were a couple of hundred feet from its summit. It was like one of those mysterious mists left over from the Mabinogion, forcing us to give in to the mountain. We walked back to the lake and along the road to the terminus of the little railway, defeated but still happy.

Shortly after I came home from the camp an incident occurred that convinced me that the shop would not last much longer. Trade, instead of 'picking up' was getting worse. Already two shops in the village had closed and the only one that seemed to be flourishing was the Co-operative. I was in the shop one Saturday morning, a time when it was previously full: now there was only a trickle of customers and most of the time it was empty. About mid-morning just after the up-train from Cardiff, a commercial traveller came in: in fact he bounced in like a terrier. He was a short, fair-haired man wearing pince-nez spectacles. His face was unfriendly and I knew that he had come about payment of a debt. After a few preliminaries he said: 'This is your last chance. If this account isn't paid by a week today, it will go out of my hands.' Father took up the end of his white apron and swept it across the polished counter, a symbolic gesture that seemed to sweep 'Pince-nez' away like the dust that was supposedly tarnishing the highly polished surface. He looked grave as the traveller threatened to give a loose rein to his anger (he had probably been sent up by his firm specially to collect the debt as Saturday was not usually a day for travellers' visits).

Father waited for him to finish, then said something like this: 'Things are difficult. I'll do my best to pay the account by next Saturday. Good morning.' Then when the traveller had gone, he told me as if nothing had happened to get the order ready for Mrs Richards, the 'Royal Oak', one of our most faithful customers.

I knew what the traveller had threatened. He would get a court order against Father if he did not pay the debt; and that would be very serious indeed. During the following week I waited for the blow to fall but nothing happened. Probably he had sold one of his properties, or possibly the bank had lent him money on the security of one of them. Whatever happened there was no upheaval, but simply the feeling—the old feeling—of a slow drifting downhill, with an occasional pause as though the slow wheels of the caravan had temporarily stopped by being bogged in a thick band of viscous mud. But we were still on the slope. The signs were unmistakable. Christmas that year was a very muted festival. In previous years I had carried a turkey or goose to Ivor Thomas so that he would bake it in his big bread-oven, as our ovens at home were too small to take a large bird. But there was no big bird this year and no brandy to burn on the Christmas pudding.

Early in the New Year, Ma went down to her home in Maesteg on a visit. I was puzzled that she had gone off at such an unseasonable time, as usually she went down to her home in the spring or the summer and took one or two of the children with her. Her eldest brother Will still lived in the old home. He was a bachelor and had a few acres of land attached to his house where he bred Welsh cobs. He also kept a thoroughbred which he raced at local races like Caerphilly, Aberpergwm and Llantrisant. But this was only a hobby; he had a responsible job in the colliery. He was 'checkweighman': he checked every 'dram', or tub, of coal at the pit-head as it came out of the cage. The collier who had cut the coal in the dram had his number plainly chalked on the outside of it: the amount of coal was entered in a ledger against his name, and his wages for the week were calculated from it. There were two men in the weighing office: one was chosen by the colliery company, the other by the colliers to represent their interest, to see that the amount of coal they had cut would be correctly recorded. Uncle Will represented the miners. He was a clean-living man, of a very serious turn of mind. He did not drink or smoke, and he was an active member of the Labour Party about seventy years ago when to be a member was to be maligned and even ostracized as a blood-thirsty revolutionary. Later in the Twenties he became chairman of the district council as did his brother George after him.

I guessed, however, that the reason for Ma's visit was not connected either with horses or with politics. The family was in a jam and she had visited him to borrow money. I never knew the result of her couple of days' visit with Uncle Will but I am pretty sure she did not come away empty-handed. He was a generous man and careless with money; he did not need much to live on and he did not value money for its own sake. His youngest sister, Averina, kept house for him, and had often told Ma that while dusting his books she had often come across twenty or thirty £1 notes, placed on the shelves among them and apparently forgotten. Yet however much the loan Ma had, it was not big enough to save the shop. In less than a month after her visit I saw her packing the family silver in a handbag. She took it to Pontypridd. When she came back without the various items, I realized we were not far from the bottom.

But a lot was to happen yet. It came about that Father was so badly in debt to wholesalers and to various firms that they would give him no more credit; and he was keeping the shop open only by buying from his fellow traders. By this time Jack had ceased to work full-time at the shop and had taken a job delivering bread for Howell Davies. I was often sent with a note and with the cart to a fellow grocer's asking him to spare a hundredweight of sugar or whatever he wanted. My feelings on these errands were very dismal. This forced me now to estimate my own position. Dinah was still at home but she was courting and would eventually get married: Esme had a job in an office but was soon to leave to become a probationer nurse. I was the oldest male still at home: should I not leave to earn my keep? But I did not want to leave school: I would get matriculation in the summer and it would be ill-advised to leave then. Besides, what would I do if I left school? With unemployment so high it would be doubtful whether I could get a job of any kind. If it were possible I would stay at school, and become either a teacher or a preacher! Neither prospect pleased but I continued to catch the 8.30 train in the morning and work at my books. Looking back I am amazed at the resilience of a sixteen-year-old who could put away all his fundamental anxieties and go on living his life as though everything was as stable and secure as the rock of a nearby hill. But again I was brought up sharply by seeing the actual avalanche that was impending.

One afternoon I saw a man in the shop: he was in earnest discussion with Father. I could not hear what they were talking about as I had just come in to fetch something; but I gathered his name was Mr Richards. He was a big, well built man with dark eyes and high cheekbones. His expression was stern and unyielding though the tone of his voice was pleasant and reasonable. I did not know what the discussion was about till Friday afternoon of that week when Father asked me to go to Aberdare on the following morning. The man I had seen, Mr Richards, was the court bailiff. He had presented a court order for payment of an outstanding debt. It could not be met until the end of the week when the few regular customers that were left paid their accounts. It was arranged that I should take the money to the court officer. I went up the valley on the school train and I had a carriage to myself and I tried to think what I myself would do if the shop was closed. But it was of no avail. The only thing to do was to live from day to day and meet each day as it came. I could not see beyond the following week and now it was useless to try.

I met Mr Richards and he was very friendly, and this eased the unpleasant job considerably so that on the way back I felt quite cheerful and said to myself: 'What the hell! That's over. Now forget about it. Next week we play at Pengam, and with luck I'll be able to have a day with the boys.' I had a strong surge of resistance: I was very active and kept myself fit. Apart from the usual games I had a more or less regular sprint to catch the train in the morning and, far less often, a sprint to catch it on the way home. It was about this time, too, that I had an experience that has never repeated itself. It was a sunny morning in June when I travelled to school as usual. I cannot remember any details of the train journey but it is probable there was the usual banter of a crowded carriage of youngsters with a sixth-former in charge keeping precarious order. This particular morning stays in the memory not because of any memorable or easily described incident but owing to the feeling I had just after I stepped out of the compartment. It was as though the weight of my body had been sloughed: I felt an intensely pleasurable lightness that took hold of my limbs: I was so relaxed that it seemed that I could float in the air and levitate in the way that eastern yogis are reputed to do. The feeling went beyond the ordinary scope of description in words: it was a subjective oneness of mind and body bound together in harmonious order. Although the experience was never repeated I later felt a vestige of it. This was a few years ahead when I was under serious training as a runner and had reached the peak of my endeavour in training for a race. Undoubtedly the kinaesthetic sense was uppermost, but my mind appeared to be as much in my muscles as in my head. It was a little like the image I experienced in dreams: of running over a flat, unencumbered plain, each stride carrying me in spectacular bounds over the landscape almost as if I were flying.

These journeys by train became a disastrous interruption in our schooling. We were always in a hurry catching trains; yet the worst feature was not the trains nor the time lost on the journey but the fact that we were distanced from the nucleus of the school community and shared only a small part in its corporate activities. Yet much amusement was to be had from the short four-mile journey. We listened to the grown-up passengers, mostly people who worked in banks, offices or shops and occasionally watched them playing cards. Sometimes we were a crowd of boys on our own, ready for fun. I recall that we had Philip Mason, a sixth-former and a good soccer player, in the compartment with us. There was not much room, and a young girl of about seventeen got in carrying a raffia basket holding a live fowl. With a nod from Mason we made place for her and she sat down after first storing her bag under the seat. He then got into conversation with her and then as blandly as though he was making a comment about the weather he said: 'I see you've got a cock between your legs this morning.'

In a rather grim contrast to the above I record that Philip Mason was dead within a couple of years after this. He went to Aberystwyth to read geography but developed tuberculosis. This was not unusual in the mid-Twenties when the effects of the 1921 strike and the consequent depression became apparent. The tubercle had already bitten deeply into the people, especially of the valleys. Two boys in the same form as I was had contracted tuberculosis and were dead before they were twenty, and there were at least four others from other forms of the school who died before they left—all victims of the same disease. At the time we were not really moved on our own behalf; we were moved by the death of our friends but we had little anxiety for our own part: T.B. was disease that someone else got, never yourself. Yet a doctor friend of mine told me years later, when I myself had a skirmish with the tubercle: 'There are few of us of our generation in the valleys that escaped the calcined scars of the disease in their lungs—the prisons or the tombs of the trapped tubercle.' The germs had attacked, but the body had fought back and had sealed them off to stop them taking over.

Abercynon

# 3 · Coal Strike and Aftermath

There was a short lull in the affairs of the shop; but it was not long before I was hearing a new word, or more properly, an 'arithmetic' word with a new meaning. The word was 'compound' and it was linked with another appearance of the court bailiff. It appeared that my father had been unable to pay a substantial debt and his creditor had obtained a court judgment against him. He had to meet this liability and pay the debt within eight days or 'compound' it to the satisfaction of his creditors, that is, pay so much of the debt, if not all of it, as his creditors had agreed. But this was not done and the dread word bankruptcy was first heard. A few days later the shop was closed. The crisis had been reached; and after being on the edge for so long Father was now at the bottom of the pit and could fall no farther. He probably felt a numb relief, at least that was my reaction, for I had long before read the signs and concluded that the business was doomed. After the news got abroad, the minister from our chapel called to see Father; I suppose, to commiserate with him. I was doing my homework in the front room, and I retreated when they entered. Logically the thought should have struck me then: 'What is the use of doing your homework? You won't be in school much longer.' But it did not. A week or so after the shop was finally closed was like the unnatural calm after a long struggle. A numbness seemed to pervade the house and each of us except Father went on with the usual household tasks. I fed the horse and was a bit sad that he would have to go in the final dispersal. But the future was out of our hands and we could only wait for things to happen. What was to follow we did not know and it was useless to rake the brain to devise a way out of the pit we had fallen into. I went on attending school and went on reading my books as though nothing had happened.

A few days later, a clerk turned up from a local auctioneer's to take a list of the stock; the few goods that were left, the scales, the warehouse equipment, the horse and the trap and the cart. It was a Saturday morning and I was free and given the job of seeing the clerk round and generally helping him to make his inventory. He was short and reticent, a bit 'superior' though only a few years older than myself. I remember the morning with deep humiliation, standing at his elbow, answering questions while he scribbled in his notebook. His questions were like fire on my skin. I had been identified with the business and had once been proud of it in my own childish way, and now it was like a grey pile of ashes.

But how did my parents take the defeat? My father seemed as impassive as ever, although, I suspect that he had deeper feelings than he was successfully able to mask. Maybe he was resigned, taking comfort in the philosophy of 'he who is down need fear no fall'. He had now 'filed his petition' and could only await the examination of his affairs in court. We as children were screened from this: as for myself, I was seized by a feeling of not caring a damn. There was even a suspension of my usual curiosity and desire to get to the bottom of things. Yet I knew my parents must have been in terrible uncertainty about the future. Where were we to live? The shop and the adjoining house would soon be sold. We heard the first murmurings of a post mortem that echoed on for years. For Ma was angry that the house we were living in had gone into the melting-pot vainly to save the business. Her temperament was the opposite from my father's. She was active and combative and took a harsh view of the whole defeat. She did not blame Father for the failure of the business: this she recognized was not his fault. The deep causes were the Depression, the shift in the predominance of the coal industry, and the different pattern of living after the war with the massive exodus of people from the area—to London, Birmingham, with some of his customers even going to the colonies and the United States. What angered Ma most of all was the losing of her home, a woman's spiritual castle, especially when she was bringing up small children. Father, she kept repeating, should have made over the house to her years ago. Other traders in the village had done this, and when a tradesman failed his wife was legal owner of the house and it could not be sold as part of the bankrupt's assets. Therefore the family had somewhere to live. What probably happened is that Father was so confident in the stability of his business, having survived a long strike before, that he estimated that the Depression would only be temporary and he could not imagine himself failing. The 1921 lock-out of the miners had destroyed his forecast; and this seemed to be confirmed by the answer he gave to Ma: 'But it was too late to make the house over. Too late. Too late.' I discovered, afterwards, that what he meant was that the business had gone downhill so fast it would have been useless to transfer some of his property because in the event of his failing the court would not recognize his making over the house to her. It had to be made at least five years before while he was still solvent.

The post-war spread of the multiple shops with their quick over-the-counter transactions and no delivery by the trader, and especially the development of the Co-operative, were undoubtedly the reasons for the failure of Father's business as of other small businesses in the valleys. Paradoxically, it was the end of the business but it was our salvation as a family. It happened like this. After the bankruptcy proceedings had been initiated, the shop and the house had been put up for auction. The Co-operative, whose premises in our street were inadequate, were the highest bidders. As it happened, Father had always been friendly with the general manager of the Co-operative, Evan Jones, as he was a nephew of one of his old friends, a north Walian who came down to work in the mines and then retired to his old home. Evan Jones had been at the auction, and when it was completed he had persuaded his committee to give Father a job, and also to allow him to live on in the house at least until the proposed opening of a butcher's that they planned to develop on its site.

This gesture was a lifeline and it was as though out of a sky of hundred per cent cloud there had appeared a cleft of light instantly followed by a brief flash of sun. We stood on firm, although much narrower, ground. We would experience a much less disastrous upheaval than we expected. We could go on more or less as we had been doing before, only with a more constricted living space and one entrance to the house instead of three. But this was a minor inconvenience in the rhythm of our lives, and it became less so as the three older members of the family left home to marry. It was our parents who bore the main burden. Father had to face the humiliation of going back to work in what was so recently his own concern. He was, however, spared the embarrassment of serving behind the counter by being placed in charge of the big warehouse at the back. He took the change in a realistic way: he had never been influenced by social gradations; and, as far as I could tell, he did not worry unduly about 'coming down in the world'. He may have actually been glad to escape from the worry of the last few years. He had, too, an understanding manager over him, and he quickly became a friend. All in all, he was as happy as he could be in such a reversal of fortune.

This experience changed my attitude towards the whole Co-operative movement. Originally I had looked upon it as a powerful rival to my father's business. But the 'Co-op's' gesture in giving him a job gave me an insight into the humane principles that informed the socialist movement. They were in business in a highly competitive society yet they did not allow a 'business' attitude to eradicate the basic humanitarian ideal that was the stimulus to the founding of the movement.

Ma's attitude to the upheaval was entirely different from Father's. Her deep motive was to stimulate her children to 'get on', to excel and rise in the social scale. In this she did not differ from thousands of Welsh mothers who wished their children to do well for themselves. They were willing to keep their children at school and, if possible, to send them to a teachers' college or to university while themselves submitted to the most punishing sacrifices. The mothers were on the whole the motivators, in working-class families at least; and I make this estimate not only from my own experience but from the experiences of my contemporaries. A close friend, Walter Gomer Rees, a miner's son whose mother kept a pub, told me one day while we were exchanging confidences (we both travelled daily to University College, Cardiff): 'I'm sure, when I get home in the evening, my old man hasn't any idea where I spend my day.' This is understandable and not nearly as flippant as might nowadays seem, for half a century ago it was not a common event, even in Wales, for a boy of twenty-one or two to stay in university without meeting some negative comment or attitude, expressed or implied. Ma's fanaticism for education was outstanding, but I am not sure whether it was for education itself or as a means to a higher step up the social ladder. I believe her attitude towards it was entirely pragmatic: she would wholeheartedly subscribe to the doctrine that was behind an oft-quoted motto: *Goreu arf arf dysg* (learning is the best weapon) rather than another that was the motto of my old school: *Deuparth bonedd yw dysg* (learning is two parts of gentility). The first was more in keeping with her combative nature. But whatever her motive, her own experiences as a child would have steeled her resolve to let her own children enjoy the best advantages she could give them. With equal justice she did not withhold her conviction in regard to her stepchildren. It was she who tried to persuade Father to let Dinah stay at school and go on to college. It was she, too, who wanted Jack, who was not gifted in the academic sense, to become apprenticed to her cousin who was a motor engineer in Cardiff. She gave the whole family her constructive and quite undemonstrative support to go as far as we could. In that she was successful. But she could never expunge her bitter memories of the failure of the shop and the struggle that followed. We heard its plaintive undersong almost to the time of her death.

As the immediate future was now settled I stayed on at school and sat the examination. I found out that if I agreed to become a teacher I could get a grant or bursary to take me through Higher Schools ('A' Level) and on to university. Even at this stage, I had doubts about committing myself to a teaching career. What I should have liked to do (this came to me when I was ten years of age) was to go about examining castles and ruins—anything to do with the past. My frequent talks with my father about his home in Y Blaenau—the foothills of the Vale of Glamorgan— and with Ivor Thomas the baker had touched a chord in my imagination, and I decided that that was what I wanted to do. I had no 'call' to be a teacher: I wanted something in the open, and found the prospect of being immured in a classroom with thirty or forty children far from attractive. But now it was the only way I could get to university at all; and I knew that I should have to jump on the teaching bandwagon, a choice that in south Wales at that time justifiably could be inscribed in large letters with the name of the renowned horse-dealer and carrier, Hobson. Its only rival was the preaching bandwagon that I suspect could similarly be labelled, but with the legend in much smaller, and more discreet, possibly gothic, characters.

Having decided the way I had to go I applied to the local council for a pupil teacher's grant just before sitting the examination that would give me exemption from another test—matriculation for entry to a university. The way ahead was clearer. But before returning for two years' study for Higher Schools, I was requested to present myself at junior school for a month's teaching practice. This was one of the conditions of the grant. The school chosen for me was Abertaf where I myself had been a pupil four years before. I was put in the charge of a young teacher called John Hughes. He was also a runner—a sprinter; and during the month I was his pupil he persuaded me that I had a turn of speed and he invited me to go training with him.

John was being trained by his half-brother Isaac (Ike) Williams, but I did not meet him until a little later. At that time, late 1925, the Miners' Welfare Ground, complete with football and cricket pitches, had not yet been constructed. There was only a rough ground near the river where football was played and nearly always occupied by a group of boys kicking a ball about. There was no smooth surface to practice running on, but the resourceful Ike had found an unusual but quiet spot. The railway to Cardiff ran alongside the river Cynon, a tributary of the Taf, and all along the line there were frequent small junctions. Wherever there was a colliery it would be linked with the main line by a short length of colliery sidings. Here three or four trains could be assembled before being fed into the main line to the coast; and the returned empty trucks stood waiting to go back to a colliery higher up the valley. All shunting on these sidings normally finished in the late afternoon, and the sidings were quiet and unfrequented. The outside tract alongside the river bank was skirted with a flat and smooth cinder path, made hard by the heavy boots of the shunters. It was a perfect surface to train on because most of the running tracks in south Wales were cinder-tracks— certainly the tracks of the professional runners. And John Hughes had been a professional since he was a boy. Up to that period there had been little tradition of amateur running in the valleys. Amateurism flourishes only in a stable environment; and it was useless in the Twenties to discuss with a miner, who was involved in frequent strikes and was earning a bare subsistence wage, the niceties of the debate between professionalism and amateurism. For him hard training and dedication deserved more than simply honour and a temporary glory, and it would be too much to expect anyone with a half empty stomach to come down on the side of amateurism. Ike Williams was a miner and himself had been a professional runner a few years before John. A 'butty' or friend of Ike's had been a runner with him and he used to come down regularly, when later I started training, to massage the runners. In my first visit to the siding John Hughes showed me how he used the track. It was too narrow for a couple of runners to compete alongside one another, and too dangerous: if one of them fell he would either collide with the coal wagons or end up in the coal-laden stream.

Life was getting fuller. During my month of pupil teaching I had been initiated into a group of young people who went about the town. Through joining the runners' school I had been invited by John Hughes to go on his evening excursions with his friends. One of the first was to the old village of Llanfabon up on the hills. Among these friends was Gwilym Williams, who had the makings of a fine pianist and was always looking for a place where there was a piano. Llanfabon was such a place. It was a typical traditional Welsh village on top of the hill, with just a church, a house opposite, and the pub. The pub had no piano, but in the house where the verger once lived I had heard the sound of one. The house had a shop in the front room: I thought a policeman lived there. It was on the route we had travelled when we were delivering goods to the farms, and I had often looked in the open door and had seen a policeman's helmet hanging in the passage. It was not until we penetrated into the house that we found that the lady who lived there was a widow and the policeman's helmet was a device to deter undesirable customers. The old lady served soft drinks; and in her middle room was a well tuned upright piano. Gwilym played well—Schubert, Beethoven, Listz—and it was a delight to listen to him.

The walks to Llanfabon were enjoyable and although the entertainment was not wildly exciting, being with 'the boys' was sufficiently satisfying. On a fine frosty night when the stars stood out like flashing diamonds and our singing voices sent out rippling waves of sound in the quiet countryside, we got a tremendous sense of expanse. In the valleys we had a limited view of the night sky; only when we got on to the hills did we understand what we were being deprived of by living down below. One night as we passed Llanfabon cemetery on our way home Joe Matthews, a young miner, put it into words: '*Duw annwyl!*' (Dear God) They put the dead 'uns on the hills where the live 'uns ought to be!' Joe was often one of the company: he had a beautiful tenor voice that could charm a bird out of a tree. When he was with us in a pub or singing walking back over the hills at night, Joe could lift our attempt at harmony to a new level, and make our day most memorable, worthy to be noted, as the old Roman said, with the whitest of white pebbles.

I have often wondered about this faculty, found in the Welsh, of being able to harmonize spontaneously, without musical training or understanding in the ordinary sense at all. This puzzled me for a long time and when I met one of the foremost authorities on folk music in Britain I asked him if he could explain the prevalence of the spontaneous love of harmony in the singing of the Welsh. His answer, as I found out later, was just 'off the top of his head': 'Oh, the Welsh learned to harmonize during the religious revival of the eighteenth century. They sang hymns which they had to learn by heart because they had no text. And of course many of them couldn't read—that, by the way, is why they repeated the last two lines of the hymns.' It was clear, however, that 'harmonizing' was a much older accomplishment than the eighteenth century. Giraldus Cambrensis, the Norman Welshman, raised the same question in the twelfth century about the Welsh love of harmony in their singing. He observed: 'In their musical concerts they do not sing in unison like the inhabitants of other countries, but in many different parts; so that in a company of singers, which one frequently meets with in Wales, you will hear as many different parts and voices as there are performers who all at length unite with organic melody in one consonance and the softness of B flat . . . and the practice is so firmly rooted in them that it is unusual to hear a simple and single melody well sung; and, what is still more wonderful, the children, even from their infancy, sing in the same manner.'

After my month of pupil teaching, I went back to the county school. The coming of the autumn and the end of the sprint training brought a new energy; but there was none of the previous year's urgency about the school work. Higher Schools was a two-year course and there was no examination at the end of the first year. There was no 'July pay', a warning phrase with which one of our masters used to berate slackers in normal years. I therefore became more aware of the girls. But I had no luck. During the first stirrings of adolescence I had admired a very dark girl of about thirteen. She was called Theda Bara after a silent screen heart-throb of the Twenties. She was intense looking and attended the central school in my home village. I sent her a note through a go-between, a classmate of hers called Frank. She never answered, for two reasons: instead of addressing her on the note as 'miss', I wrote what must have appeared to her as 'mips' before her name. I had copied it from letters I had posted for my father who was still using the old fashioned form of the internal 's'. Worse still I had included with the note a bar of scented soap I had stolen from the shop. The next time I saw Frank he told me she was deeply offended: 'What was that you called her? And it was a bit daft sending her scented soap, wasn't it? She thought you hinted she looked scruffy.'

I was glad to get back to school. I had now been smitten by a tall fair-haired girl. Yet when I got back to Mountain Ash I heard that she and her family had gone to India where her father had an appointment as a mining engineer. I felt sorry for myself and wrote a lament in very halting Welsh verse, the only language I felt could carry my true feelings. But there were plenty of other girls around and there were opportunities to meet them, apart from in class. We had a short dance every Friday afternoon in the new hall for about three quarters of an hour after school. My first girl's place was soon filled by a dark girl from two forms below mine who did not attend the dancing class. I had noticed her in school, but it was not until I had seen her on the same platform as Lloyd George that I felt she was desirable. She was in the front row of a welcoming choir that sang while the audience awaited his arrival. Her features were typically Celtic: broad forehead, curving to a pointed chin—a heart face. The great man was speaking in the old Eisteddfod Pavilion at a political meeting. There was still industrial turmoil that was to lead eventually to the 1926 General Strike. The vast hall was packed with hundreds of miners up to the gallery that towered above the huge floor. Lloyd George's wartime glamour had sadly waned—and the miners were in a critical mood. They spent their time singing—not hymns but secular and satirical songs like *Crawshaw Bailey's Engine*, with abrasive choruses. But when he arrived, after the welcoming thunder that came from the floor of the hall, there was a silence that the Wizard used to divine the predominant feeling of the audience, and to pitch his note accordingly. It was a dramatic example of what came to be known later as 'charisma'—this short white-haired gentleman in a morning suit, his white locks like those pictured in gothic representations of Merlin, or one of the early bards, giving his large head the look of a prophet about to give utterance. He stood perfectly still, in silence, inviting the hostility that he sensed from the gallery, challenging it to break out in imprecation or abuse. The silence remained unbroken and he began his speech in his own time, and apart from a few interruptions that he either ignored or countered with a sharp rapier-like response, his short, emotive twenty-minute speech ended with a typical dramatic peroration. Its burden was that the difficulties before us were menacing and not easily to be surmounted, but we must not be dismayed—and so on, and so on. Then after a few rolling periods his head went back and he pointed high to the farthest corner of the Pavilion as if he had seen a vision, his foot forward and his hand outstretched, working to his climax in a Welsh *hwyl*:

Hawdd yw dywedyd, Dacw'r Wyddfa
Ond nid eir drosti ond yn ara'.

Easy to say, yonder's Snowdon,
But slow's the path across it.

The applause was thunderous; and while it continued, Lloyd George raised his arm in quasi benediction, and hurriedly left the platform with the audience in stunned silence as though they were wondering what had caused the uproar.

My dark girl's choir sang a valedictory chorus that relieved the tension but left me staring at her. She had been transformed: she was a different creature that had suddenly bloomed in the Wizard's brilliance. Yet even in my impatience to get out and meet her at the stage door, a still, cold voice made itself heard: 'This isn't real love. You must be a hollow snob to desire a girl just because she has stood within the spotlight of the Great.' I now suspect that this instability is a common affliction, observed by a seventeenth-century writer, John Aubrey, who had expertly charted the course of the wandering barque of adolescence. Out of his long experience he held: 'The only time for learning is from nine to sixteen; afterwards Cupid begins to tyrannize.' It was certainly an observation that was right for me; although the arrows did not penetrate far, they were often shot and I could well have been deeply wounded before I had reached the age of twenty.

In spite of the unpromising future, this was a cheerful time. I was free from the worries of the shop and I was now also free to travel as a regular member of the School XV to play against other schools on a Saturday morning. We were trying desperately to keep up the reputation of a team that had two International caps in it. They had played in the Welsh Secondary XV that had been newly formed. Although the running practice had discontinued for the time being I still did the running-on-the-spot exercise that Ike had advised. In the evenings I went out occasionally with John Hughes and his posse of 'bloods'. Sunday was the big rallying time. After chapel the young people made for the regular parade—the main road between Abercynon and Cilfynydd, the next village to the south where the Taf valley opened out. There was not much motor traffic in the Twenties and the young people took virtual possession of the road. In the summer they paraded along a disused railway cutting at the foot of Craig Evan Leyshon in twos and threes of their own sex, usually passing one another in good humoured raillery a few times during an evening, perhaps singing out to each other till they 'clicked'; that is, until they had stopped and talked to a couple of the opposite sex. On one boy's initiative, he would pair off with the girl of his choice and his companion would take the other. Then they would stroll off in tandem, taking the girls home. If they got on together they would make 'points', appointments, arranging to meet on a future occasion, not singly but as the original group. The parents would only allow a girl out if she had a companion; and as long as a girl could say, 'I'm going for a walk with Betty after chapel,' everything would be in order. The girl could say this truthfully although the sequel to the walk with Betty would mean their splitting up. But it was all very innocent and unsophisticated. The influence of the home and of the chapel was too strong for any deep, sexual involvement. Moreover, for the boy if he had any aspiration to get to a university, it would be disastrous if he became involved with a girl and made her pregnant. He would immediately be excommunicated from the chapel; and any career he had mapped out for himself would be blighted at the start. This was a real deterrent against pre-marital sex; and once you had seen the effect of the breaking of the prohibition you were not disposed, however much you liked a girl, to risk having your name read out in chapel and thus suffering a public humiliation.

Many visitors not familiar with the valleys in the Twenties and Thirties interpreted such parades of young people as a 'loose' relationship between the sexes. In fact, the relation was easy, and rarely loose, and in the long run was far better than the decorous and nervous circumspection that existed in some cultures. Co-educational schools, that were almost the rule in the valleys, with the free mixing of the sexes as at house parties, were a much better training for after-school life than the segregated schools that seemed to be the rule in the anglicized towns, like Cardiff and Newport where a commercial middle class opted for copies of the old English grammar and public schools' systems.

Often, however, I forgot about girls and took long walks on the hills either by myself or with a school friend, Jack Sugarman. After spending some days in the valleys I became restless and longed to get on to the hills. I felt freer on the hills and responded to their austere beauty. So that even fifty years later, after seeing many much vaunted and acclaimed beautiful spots to which I can freely give an intellectual assent, nothing moves me so much as the bare unencumbered skyline of a Welsh hillside. The Glamorgan Hills spoke to me as no other scene has spoken to me since. It was possible at that time to see the evidences of the past that had so absorbed me from my childhood. Most of the ancient traces in the valley had been wiped out by the flood of industrialism, a much earlier tide than commonly thought. As far back as the sixteenth century, the Cynon valley had been denuded of its woodlands to make charcoal for iron smelting and for ship-building, a nascent industry under the Tudors. An anonymous contemporary poet wrote bewailing the spoliation:

Aberdar, Llanwnna i gyd;
plw Merthyr hyd Llanfabon;
Mwya adfyd a fu erioed
pan dorred coed Glyn Cynon.

Aberdare, Llanwynno—down
from Merthyr to Llanfabon;
a greater blow was never seen
than cutting the woods of Cynon.

Our neighbours across the border got the blame for it, and the poet in his anger wrote: *Ynghrog y byddo'r Saeson* (Let the Saxon be hanged). The same thing was happening in north Wales where a contemporary poet, Robin Clidno, was writing about a similar loss in a more subtly worded protest. He made it through the mouths of a band of little squirrels led appropriately by a splendid red matron who took them in a deputation to London where she put their case before the 'Council'. The red matron represented them eloquently and finished her appeal with a Parthian shot that has a modern significance:

Gwir a ddywed Angharad:
Oni cheir glo, yn iach i'n gwlad.

Truly spake our friend Angharad;
Farewell to our country if we don't get coal.

Dyffryn Court

# 4 · *The New School and Rugby*

On Tuesday, 4 May 1926, the General Strike began, as was expected, and the train taking us to school did not run. My friend 'Niblo' Robinson and I walked the four miles to school. I recall vividly my state of mind on that May morning. It was a bright day but we walked up the valley, not on its comparatively rural side, but along the side where most of the houses were. We wanted to see if there was any excitement. Apart from an occasional front door being open and a couple of the women chatting there were no men about. My mood was rebellious. It was not that we had a real consciousness of what was at stake: it was a vague, undefined 'agin the government' impulse that caused us to spend most of the morning on the road instead of being at school. We had been infected by the prevailing mood and were cocking an ineffective and harmless snook at authority.

But that day was memorable for me in that a period of intense unease and conflict set in. I was trying to see clearly through a dilemma I could not solve. For when the shop closed it seemed to be expected of me that I should now leave school and earn a living. Nothing was said by my parents although they had probably discussed it. But what sort of a job could I get? And why should I get a job when I had better prospects through staying at school? A kind of stubbornness and a streak of hardness or pure selfishness tipped the balance of the moral dilemma that, if I had been able to state it, would have been: 'What am I if I think only of myself and not of others? Yet who is for me if I am not for myself?' I felt that Ma would be on my side if I decided to stay at school, and finally I resolved the problem merely by walking round it; and the prospect of a bursary helped me in my decision. But on this day at the start of the General Strike, I must have had a premonition of what would happen. The miners stayed out after the general resistance folded up. The pulse of trade in the valleys slowed up almost to inanition. As the weeks of the strike went by the Co-operative was affected by the falling away of demand and they were compelled to put their employees on short time. Father now worked four days a week; and this renewed the old conflict: should I remain at school while things were becoming difficult at home?

Yet in spite of the persistent unease I travelled to school and took an active part in school life, though I got the reputation among the staff of being lazy. This was indeed true, for while the strike was on I had slacked off book-work, not knowing whether or not I should be able to return to finish the course during the following year. But again a dry summer helped people to ride out the difficult time. For although the weather was not as halcyon as the last big strike of 1921, it was memorable for its spells of sunny days. The out-of-work miners again organized activities that the fine weather favoured. At Ynysybwl, over the hill, they dammed up the Clydach, a small stream, and formed a swimming pool where they spent the sunny afternoons. They also held sports meetings, chiefly foot-races and whippet racing, wherever they could find a flat piece of ground to hold them. The older men spent their time on their allotments as they did during the 1921 lock-out, extending them wherever they could; and that year the farmers had plenty of help to gather in the hay harvest.

Much of my time out of school that summer I spent with Ike Williams and his school of runners. For the thought had entered my mind that if I trained and managed to win a handicap during the following year it would be a positive step in getting to a university. Ike had a good school of runners and now he had plenty of time to give to them. His one aim was to get a runner to 'do even time', that is to run a hundred yards in ten seconds, which was the goal over a half-century ago. If a runner could get near that speed he was bound to pick up some money. The two important handicaps in the valleys at that time were the Cambrian Dash and the Welsh Powderhall, run in the early summer and August respectively. The stakes were high, and it was Ike's plan to train a runner for each of these as well as the numerous local handicaps. Llewellyn Jenkins, the star runner in Ike's school, was admirably built for a sprinter: he was stocky with a good muscle coverage and he had dedication. It was necessary to practise starts continually, as quickness out of the holes was of first importance in a short sixty-yard dash. I could hold Llew for about twenty yards from the start: after that he pulled quickly away; but that was all we needed for starting practice, a series of quick bursts from the Dick Turpin pistol that Ike held. He started the race in the approved, professional manner, one foot well forward, the gun held up firmly with both hands and pointing well above our head. Oftentimes, he put so much powder in the barrel that the explosion reverberated in the hills. But while practising starts he normally used the starting pistol with the much milder explosion of a small cap.

In my last year at school I became a member of the Baptist chapel next door to the shop. Later, after reacting against its narrowness, I began to value its positive side. Most of the members were sincere—they had been through a very searing fire; and although I could not subscribe to some of their values, they did hold a guiding rein on young people starting out in their first experiments with life. The chapel, too, offered companionship with boys of my own age, who would go out together in the informal parade after service on a Sunday evening; often on a dark winter evening walking on the mountain road, singing secular songs, although finishing up with hymns that were not sung with any particular devotion but because we liked the tunes with their harmony, especially the tenor parts and the rolling or rumbling in the bass. Chapel society frequently gave amusement and sometimes embarrassment, especially when we heard the more evangelical praying and uttering of fundamentalist sentiments that even an immature youth could dismiss as fantasy. One of the elders, for example, would hold forth with strict sabbatarian zeal; and one day he surpassed himself by saying that going to the seaside on a Sunday instead of going to chapel was no better than skirting the sands of Hell. This brought up an incongruous picture: instead of beautiful, svelte houris skirting the dunes, weaving to and fro in their lightly clad voluptuousness, big fat women with their dresses tucked into their bloomers, such as we would often see when we went on the Sunday school treat to Porthcawl or Barry Island, lolloping along the water's edge and screaming with feigned terror as they got their feet wet.

Swearing was another abomination to the chapel deacons. At least half of them worked in the pit and heard a surfeit of it in the course of their daily work, both in Welsh and in English. Their dilemma underground was highlighted by one of the chapel members who was not himself a deacon. He was known by the nickname of Tom 'Murphy'.

He was not Irish but almost monoglot Welsh and got his name because of his disguising the common Welsh expletive *Myn Uffern i* (by Hell), metamorphosing it into 'Murphy', the initial element of a string of innocuous expletives that could be added to according to the nature of the provocation: 'Murphy, Mahogany, Bull, Dutch, Madagascar, Connecticut', and so on. I had never heard my father swear in anger. Sometimes in humorous exasperation he would come out with a Welsh oath *'R Asgwrn Dafydd'* (By the bone of St David) which had an interesting ring about it: St David was celebrated on 1 March but he was never invoked officially in Welsh nonconformity; and the oath was almost certainly a pre-Reformation survival.

Back at school, notwithstanding my settling down to work at my books, there was still doubt pricking at my mind. For the lock-out still continued well into the autumn. But then suddenly it ended. The miners had lost their battle in the long struggle against the coal-owners and they had been forced to return to work, subdued and constrained to admit a temporary defeat. The Co-operative stores, now that the lock-out was over, went back to normal and my father worked a full week. My bursary as a pupil teacher also came through and I was able to buy a much needed suit of clothes and a pair of shoes. This was the era of the 'fifty-shillings tailor' when you could buy a suit for that amount, and a pair of shoes for under a pound. I recall that I bought a very colourful pullover with a stylized Egyptian design that had become popular after the discovery of the Tutankhamun tomb. I wore the pullover to school, and shortly afterwards we had a little homily from the 'boss' during morning assembly about some of the older boys wearing clothes with carnival colours to school. There was no regulation school-dress, at least for the boys. The girls wore gym-slips and the boys were expected to wear clothes of a serviceable dark hue. It was just as well that dress for the boys was not prescribed during the penurious Twenties, for while the girls' slips could be tailored at home, homemade clothes for boys were a different matter.

A new suit of clothes armoured me with a hopeful feeling that covered over the recent doubts. There was, too, a hopeful atmosphere about the school itself: having recently moved away from what was an educational slum, we were now in a beautiful island in the valley. The house and park belonged to an old-established Welsh family that preceded the Bruces who turned the house into Plas y Dyffryn (Dyffryn Court) about 1750; and it had a little of the graciousness of the eighteenth-century houses that are so frequently to be found in England. It was built on a platform that sloped gently down to the river Cynon, two or three hundred yards away. It had the usual features of the country house of that period: a well kept lawn at the front, trees and shrubs behind and at the side, and a ha-ha that divided a long meadow at the front of the house but did not obstruct the view over it.

Most pleasant of all was the new relaxed atmosphere of the school. It was true that as we had reached our last year we had privileges and were in an entirely different position, but even so the temper of the school had changed appreciably, and a great deal of this was due to the new surroundings. We had made a new start; and both children and teachers were happier. In the sixth form we ceased to be treated as children; and we became friendly with the staff, and out of this contact the teachers' points of view permeated through to us, distancing us in some degree from the junior forms.

Harries Jones, the Latin master, was taking three of us through Higher Schools and one afternoon he came into the form-room to take us for an hour in Tacitus' *Agricola*. Something was up: we could see he was disturbed by the way he entered the room. He stood for a moment before the desk and threw the book down on it. Then he sat down, and as he opened the text of the *Agricola* he told us with a restrained vehemence: 'If any of you are thinking of taking up this job, think hard and look for something else.' Hywel Harries Jones came from north Wales. He was dark skinned and of a slim athletic build. As a schoolboy he had played half-back at soccer and he had got his cap for Wales, but that was about twenty years before. He was a good teacher who took music as well as his main subject. The outbreak was surprising and atypical; and I remembered what one teacher had told me during teaching practice of his attitude towards his work: 'Some days you are happy and think you are doing a worthwhile job; other days I wonder what in Hell's name I am doing wasting my time here.' Perhaps it was one of Harries Jones's off-days, but it made me consider, having witnessed the utter sincerity of his outburst.

Another teacher, Alys Evans, the history mistress, shortly afterwards asked me what I was going to read at university and what I intended doing afterwards. I explained my plan of going into teaching as it was the only way of getting to university at all; but after a few years' teaching I would get out and take another job. She told me: 'There's one thing you'll have to beware of, and that's 'the Rut'. Once you begin teaching you get into 'the Rut'; and it's very hard indeed to get out of it.' Alys Evans spoke with conviction as though out of her own experience. She

had a fine soprano voice which we sometimes heard at house parties,
and possibly she had thought of developing it and making singing her
career. If so, she had come to terms with her disappointment and was
now a dedicated teacher who did everything to help us in our course.
For example, our greatest trouble in history was to come by the
expensive text books. When I first went to the county school we had to
buy our own books, but shortly after the 1921 stoppage in the mines the
county council decided to supply them free. It was doubtful whether the
valley schools could have operated otherwise in the years that followed.
Even so, for Higher Schools, especially in history, we needed a wide
range of textbooks to cover a course that included medieval as well as
modern history, with the French Revolution as a period of special study.
There were no public libraries in the valleys in the Twenties. There
were the Miners' Institute Libraries in most villages, many of them good
ones, specializing in subjects that mainly concerned the miners, such as
socialism, religion, economics, philosophy and mining itself. The
miners contributed so many pence a week from their wages towards the
founding and upkeep of their institutes; and it was only fair that the
facilities—of the library at least—should be confined to the miners and
their families. A non-miner had to pay to become a member of the
library. In these circumstances Alys Evans used to borrow books, on her
own initiative, for her small group of history students. She lived in the
valley during the week but went home to Cardiff at the weekend,
bringing back a much needed book she had borrowed from Cardiff
Public Library for her three students to read. Such a book was Alexis de
Tocqueville's *The Ancient Regime and the French Revolution*. I was
engrossed by this book which came like manna from Heaven. I can still
read it with something of the excitement of reading it for the first time;
and I can still marvel at its penetrating insights. By the time Alys Evans's
three students had read the book, the fines she had to pay must have
been considerable.

Another of our teachers who were concerned with our general
welfare was Ethel James who had taken us in English during the
previous years. She was a farmer's daughter from Pembrokeshire. She
was sociable and outgoing, and had adapted herself immediately to the
life in the mining valley that became a second home to her. Shortly after
the school moved to Dyffryn House she became senior mistress, and set
herself both to ease the transition to the new site and to introduce new
activities that it made possible. One of these proved very popular: it was
a weekly dancing class for the fifth and sixth forms. It was held for an

hour or so on Friday afternoon immediately after school, and a group of about twenty usually stayed. It was a kind of revolutionary gesture for there was a strong chapel feeling against dancing, partly due to the fear of 'what happens after the ball'; but Ethel James managed to persuade the head, who was a reasonable family man, that it was a desirable innovation, and it was very successful. It gave us something to look forward to and made a good end to the week: it helped to bring a much needed balance to our view of school as somewhere humdrum with a 'life-is-earnest' message that got very boring. It also helped to give us boys, at least, a bit of social polish which was somewhat lacking in our dealings with girls: it taught us to approach them with confidence and formally to ask them to dance—a ritual that was still practised in those days—and to pilot them around the floor with assurance. This provided a useful skill when we attended dances later on; and we escaped the late initiation that many of those boys from segregated schools suffered when they got to college.

School rugby outings were tremendous morale-boosting occasions. Usually one of the masters would go with us. We travelled to Cardiff, Swansea and various schools in the valleys: Pontypridd, Merthyr, the Rhondda, Aberdare and so on. But there was extra enjoyment in visiting new places and in travelling back home with a group that had been lit up by a good game and burst into song at the slightest impulse. On one occasion during my first year in the sixth we played at Pengam, a school that had just changed from soccer to rugby. After the match while waiting on a Saturday afternoon for a train at Bargoed station to take us back home, the team started to sing. The opposite platform was crowded with shoppers. They appeared glad to listen, and clapped appreciatively after one of our songs. So we proceeded to give the crowd an improvised concert including *Calon Lân* which we adopted as our school song, since the writer of the words lived in Mountain Ash. This was much to the enjoyment of the crowd until our train came in and ended it. But this singing after a rugby match was an established tradition in south Wales. Immediately after the match the singing would start in the dressing-room—particularly if we had won!—and would continue sporadically during the evening and on the way home.

The singing tradition was particularly vigorous at Mountain Ash because of a successful male voice choir led by Glyndwr Richards. The town was lucky in having a National Eisteddfod Pavilion, a solid structure of huge proportions left over from the 1905 visit of the Eisteddfod to the town. This pavilion became a centre for singing in the valley, and the Mountain Ash choir had an excellent venue for its concerts. In the early Twenties I recall Glyndwr Richards bringing his choir back from their tour of the United States. As a boy I heard them singing pieces that have become a large part of the repertoire of male voice choirs in Wales: *Y Delyn Aur, Myfanwy, Cyfrif'r Geifr, O Mor Ber Yn Y Man, The Soldier's Chorus, Crossing the Plain.* The brief period after the First World War, before the Depression set in, was a golden age of Welsh choirs. There was one in nearly every village in the valleys and competition was intense. But for a long time afterwards the choirs lived under the shadow of that period, content to sing the old favourites, eschewing innovation and bowing more to nostalgia than attempting any fresh ventures in song.

After training for sprinting during the summer months, I enjoyed playing rugby with the school team. We played on most Saturday mornings during the first two terms, and we collected a fairly good record. This was at a time when the Welsh secondary schools were changing over, almost without exception, to rugby football, and some of our fixtures were against teams who were experiencing their first terms of rugby. The Welsh Secondary Schools' Rugby movement had recently been started and had begun their series of 'international' matches against France and the Yorkshire secondary schools—two fixtures that were the forerunners of the full international programme that later developed. This new movement bore very early fruit, for it was the alumni of the Welsh Secondary movement who were the stars in a revival of the Welsh team that beat New Zealand at Cardiff in 1935.

In the early Twenties the Mountain Ash Club—known locally as 'the Old Firm'—had a team of good standing and you could see many of the outstanding Welsh Clubs play on 'the Rec', the ground that had been laboriously hewn out of the rock that formed the west side of the valley. Yet the club was affected by the economic malaise that quickly spread over the valley, especially after the 1926 strike. Many of their promising players, mostly miners, had no choice but to listen to the offers they were getting from Northern Union clubs, and there was a mass exodus north from many of the valley clubs, a movement that affected the national side as well as the contributory local clubs. But before its decline 'the Old Firm' had a good record and there was a corresponding keenness in the school. It was exhilarating to play in the three-quarters at that time, before the studied development of wing-forward obstruction dampened the exuberance of back-play; or at least before it had reached the schools. It was a great thrill, from the wing or centre position to coast at speed and accelerate with the ball under the arm in an ecstatic dash for the try-line. Afterwards, from the late twenties and most of the Thirties, the wing-forward destroyed the classical back play so favoured by the Welsh; and the wing three-quarters was often left for a whole game without handling the ball except to throw it in from touch during a line-out.

In my last term at school we competed in a relay race against a school from one of the coastal towns, and we won. There was at least one professional runner in our team—a boy who had competed and won a professional handicap. In the 'English' towns along the Glamorgan coast there was only one form of athletics known to their boys at school—amateurism. Therefore there was no temptation to succumb to professionalism. The valleys and the coastal towns were two different cultures: the newly sprung-up port towns, fostered by the Industrial Revolution, developed along the English middle-class pattern; the valley towns, by and large, had a Welsh peasant substratum and a proletarian overlay. The divide between professional and amateur was largely academic in the valleys for the reason that during the Depression, the want—and indeed almost absolute poverty—showed that only one code had a meaning. The distinction between codes was blurred, necessarily. If you played rugby you would be expected to be paid 'expenses' at this time and the term was generously interpreted. Moreover, it was a human interpretation never felt by most amateurs at the time: briefly, it was a natural need for money to live a less straitened life. At least this incident of a professional running with amateurs made me think of an issue that I had hardly considered: so desperate was I for money that I had given the moral issue little thought. Yet before the end of the afternoon something occurred that settled the issue for me; so excited was I at our team's success that, in ducking under the barbed wire that separated the field from the changing area, I badly tore my jacket. (There were no track suits in those days; at least we didn't have any.) The jacket was part of the only suit I possessed; if I wanted to get to college I would have to get a new one. It was impossible to get a vacation job, and if I wanted to go to college I had to win a handicap. For even if I passed the examination I was then sitting—which I was pretty sure of doing—and gained admission to College I would not have the teachers' grant for some weeks after I had started the term.

In a certain class of society it was the convention, or rather fantasy, never to mention money; to pretend it did not exist, although it was then virtually the be-all and end-all of existence at our level. For the next two months money was to be my abiding thought, night and worrying day. If becoming a real professional runner made it possible for me to get to college I was prepared to lose caste. If it meant being looked down on by the amateurs; if it meant becoming a proletarian, so be it. I had come from a working-class background and the simple desire to 'better myself' did not mean that I was going to desert it.

In the meantime the school term was coming to an end. The result of the examination would be out at the end of August. All my thought was to earn enough money to fit myself out with a suit. It is ironic to consider how dated and pretentious this now appears. Today, a student needs only a pair of cheap jeans and a pullover to present himself for registration; and successive pairs of jeans and pullovers will see him through college. But fifty-five years ago, although the received dress for students was a pair of flannels, or 'Oxford bags', and a sports jacket, he found a lounge suit a necessity for interviews with headmasters he might come into contact with; and if he wished to take an active part in the social life of the college he would be compelled to invest in a dinner jacket even if it was one that cost only a few pounds. Again, I was not in a position to pay for lodgings near the university college where I had been accepted, therefore I would have to travel the fifteen miles to Cardiff by train. This meant a term's season ticket to be bought before the term began. I estimated that about £15 would see me through until my grant was paid.

With this figure in mind I approached Ike Williams and told him of my wish to enter for a handicap to try and get some money to equip myself for the college term. But Ike was evasive: he wanted me to 'work up a mark', to go slowly and then try for a big handicap during the following year. Working up a mark meant a studied policy of entering handicaps and not winning them. This ploy of beating the handicapper was one of the most doubtful aspects of professional running. If you did not show your full pace for a few races it was possible to get a better mark, and with a good mark you could choose your handicap and, theoretically, you would have a good chance of winning it. But there were more shady practices of building up a mark. For example, some trainers had a special pair of running spikes made: they were fitted with a thin plate of lead in the insole of each foot and expertly concealed. The total weight of the lead was as much as half a pound, and when he was wearing these shoes a runner showed yards slower than his true form. Another trick was to give a runner a pair of shoes that was a size or two too small for him so that he ran in his heat with a slightly cramped foot that would automatically retard him. Then in the semi-final or final, having barely scraped home in spite of the disability, he wore his usual shoes, had increased odds and would win the prize for himself and a good haul for his backers.

I was aware of the underhand practices that went on in professional running, analogous I suppose to the taking of drugs by modern sportsmen; but so desperate was I to get my objective that I dismissed the shady practices to the nether part of my mind—I would win a handicap to get myself out of present difficulties and then give it up. I knew at the time that a professional runner was considered by amateurs as one of the lesser breeds. But 'needs must'. I had set my mind on a certain course and I had to accept all its implications. There was another consideration that weighed against my waiting to build up a mark and leave winning a handicap until the following season. I did not enjoy the prospect of patiently attending a string of meetings with boring regularity. The main excitement in a foot-race event of this kind was with the punters, exactly as in horse-race meetings. Invariably foot-race events were held in conjunction with whippet-racing; and every time the starting gun went off there would be a furious and strident barking and howling of dogs so that each event, foot or whippet, was run against a loud cacophony of sound that coloured the whole afternoon.

The season was now advancing quickly and I would have to enter a handicap if I wanted to get to university at all. I therefore decided to run in a handicap with another boy who was at school with me and who was dissatisfied with this temporizing. He was about to join the R.A.F. and wanted money for the same reason as I did. We entered a race held at Llantrisant on a bank holiday, and although it was a pleasant day we won nothing.

A few weeks later during August I was entered for a valleys event, a £20 handicap at Merthyr Vale. It was an uncertain afternoon with showers of rain, a real valleys' day when the gloom of the hills is enhanced by the lack of sun. But I was happy running in the rain: somehow the patter of the warm drops of rain seemed to relax my muscles, at any rate it stimulated me to win my heat. The semi-final was comfortable; and we ran the final in a sharp shower. I was in my proper element and I won by two yards. The prize was £15—over seven weeks' wages for a collier in 1927, and for me a small fortune. My worries were over for the time being. A week later I heard that I had passed my examination, getting my three subjects and winning a bursary on the overall result. The way ahead was brighter than it had been for years.

Nothing was going to stop me now.

In the meantime, preparations for the rugby season had already started and I was asked by Harry Mills, the school rugby star, who had already been playing for 'the Old Firm' for a season, to turn out for a practice match at their ground in preparation for the first match. I played in this game and was surprised to hear that I was selected to play in the first home match against Pontypool. I had been thrown in at the deep end, playing my first game in senior rugby against a first-class club and marking an international wing, Cliff Richards. Had I known it, by accepting to play in this game, I had unconsciously chosen the course of my life for the next four years. Even before my entry to university I became identified with a certain group, and I remained with them until I left. For at the start of the term I met some of the boys we had played against during the previous couple of seasons at school; and although I had missed the college trial match I was asked to join the college team that was to become my centre of interest while I was at university. I had been type-cast, a privileged member of the rugby team almost before I had entered; and although I was not completely happy in the role, it was a flattering one and gave me some badly needed assurance. Having no real guidance I had fitted into the niche that first offered itself. My immediate purpose had been to get into university, but my aim was not settled: I did not know what I wanted to do ultimately. I had opted to teach because it was the only way out of the valley; and I had some idea of getting out of teaching after a few years. But this was so vague and so far in the future that essentially I was ready to drift, to coast along partly in the relief reaction to what had happened at home during the past few years. Yet essentially I lacked a definite goal. I had no urge to become a scholar and to bury myself in academic life; on the other hand I was not completely happy in the guise of a 'hearty'. The trouble was that I was an odd mixture of extrovert and introvert, predominantly an outward looker at this period of my life, alternating with short intervals of dreamy and not very flattering inward examination. I was the pattern of a divided man forever functioning on half-power who was perforce getting by with a pale copy of what he had the potential to be. Yet this conflict in retrospect was an inevitable part of my individual growth. My personal difficulties—mainly the asthma that I kept a secret from everybody—precluded any tendency I had to look within and attempt to solve them. For it is infinitely easier to face things that are outside yourself than wrestle with the deep limitations within, the snags and burrs that you are aware of but cannot locate. That, I feel sure, was the reason why at this time almost all my energy became focused on rugby football and the related social side of college life.

But these are backward promptings, a personal estimate that pays little regard to what is in fact a collective aspiration. Why was it that I was so obsessed with rugby football? I was only, after all, one of a community, of a society that for the past century or so had elevated rugby football into becoming a symbol of itself as a nation. It is true that a kind of traditional rough and tumble game had been played in Wales, as in other parts of Britain occupied by the Celts, a game of hacking and hustling an object from one end of the village to the other. Yet the spring for the spate of enthusiasm for rugby was more specific. To win at the game, especially against England, is as important as gaining victory in the long war Wales began fighting for its independence centuries ago.

No one can understand the seriousness that is paid to rugby in Wales unless he views it as a social and political affirmation of its nationhood. For a nation that has existed for many years as subject to a more powerful one it is the sheet-anchor of its self-respect. And this 'powerful one' is something more than a nation: down the years it has become a nation-state, a nation expanding itself and by aggrandizement absorbing the small nations near it into its imperial self, expunging the little clans and calling the new unit—as a sop to their sense of identity—Great Britain. It is yet a small nation's philosophy to be left alone, to assert its own individuality, that has been nurtured during its long history by its refusal to sink itself into the abstract mass of another people. It is aware this can only be a shadow, a pale, political reflection unless it retains its language, the one asset that can make it a true nation. At no other time has there been such an insidious attack on the small nations that are considered lets and hindrances to the development of the modern world. The nation-state, which is fundamentally commercial, penetrates all corners of the world. It takes up the stance: how much easier it would be if we all had a common language, how much more pleasant to have commerce with one another when 'commerce' is the only thing that matters, the god that we must all bow down to.

I could not blame my young self too much for my interest in rugby football, especially in a valley community. For here I had an inkling of how rugby had become the Welsh national game, in the double sense, when I saw my first international—Wales against England—at the Arms Park in 1927. There was a strong contingent from west Wales and I call to mind a group from Llanelli easily distinguishable by their scarlet scarves, marching from the railway station to the ground. They had a champion to support—Albert Jenkins the famous Llanelli centre—and they were chanting, as they went along, the ancient cry *'Lan i chi Cymry, Lan i chi Cymry'* ('Up the Welsh'), a cry that was undoubtedly old enough to hearten Henry Tudor as he led the Welsh contingent to Bosworth Field. Again, about this time, I saw how strong it was in a second generation Englishman, Fred Weston, a big fair-headed forward who played in the college team. The yeast of nationhood was still working in the valleys in spite of the inundation by an alien population when the Industrial Revolution got under way. At first there was the inevitable clash between peoples of a different culture; but gradually there arose a new spirit of a nation centred consciously on prowess at rugby football, so that within a couple of generations the sons of incomers to the valleys had identified with the Welsh Rugby Team. Fred Weston's father had come from over the border to work in the steelworks at Ebbw Vale and later Port Talbot, and his son graduated at Cardiff and became a French master at a grammar school in the Thames Valley. He later confessed to us that he was an Englishman in Wales but once in England his reactions were transposed. He became more Welsh than the Welsh. But I suspect that a great deal of his 'Welshness' was a social reaction. He contrasted the freer and warmer community of Ebbw Vale and Aberavon where he was brought up with the stiff, hierarchical strata of southern England; and he was forced to confess his preference.

Undoubtedly, I myself looked upon going to college as an escape from an impossible situation at home. Whether this was due to the unstable background of the last few years or to weakness of character, my one desire was to enjoy myself in the circumstances that offered. Logically, since I had got to university by the skin of my teeth, my one resolve should have been to work hard at my books and aim for a first class degree. Yet my heart was not in academic distinction and I, or my own particular daimon, had made that negative choice. Shortly after starting on the first year courses we had to vacate the house that had been our family home, as the Co-operative wanted to convert it into a branch of their butchery department. We moved into a council house. And although the elder members of the family had married and left home the new house was very crowded, and it was next to impossible to study with any concentration in such conditions. I hadn't the funds to lodge in Cardiff and therefore had to waste time in travelling. In the upshot, I could waste more time doing other heedless things than going to and fro on the fifteen miles to Cardiff.

# 5 · College

The first days at college were chaotic and rather an anticlimax. They were taken up mainly with signing up for the various courses you intended taking in your first year. This meant waiting about for an interview with the senior lecturer of the department—sometimes, it seemed interminably—before you could see him. In addition to my degree subjects it was also necessary for me to see the Professor of Education who supervised students entering college on a Board of Education grant. He was rather a self-important little man with a loud voice. He was a resounding example of the saying that a small man makes up in 'consequence' what he lacks in inches. He was the funnel of entry for the majority of boys who came from the valleys—the watchdog at the gate—and the queue outside his room was a long one. He dealt with the entrants himself, not like the professors in the other departments who left it to their subordinates. We were called in in pairs to save time; and it turned out that we had to make an attestation. It was a Board of Education fiat that each intending graduate who had accepted its assistance in going through college had first to swear that he would in fact enter the profession once he had qualified. The ritual was a bit like that for entering the armed forces, as I later found out. It is true there was no swearing on the Bible, but each of us had to suffer the minatory stare of the short professor and attest by reading out a formula from a card that we undertook to follow a course of post-graduate training and to teach for a minimum number of years—I forget how many—once we had qualified. The professor's histrionics touched off my asthma and I stumbled through the formula. I got out of the room as soon as I could and dismissed the ceremony from my mind. An instinct seemed to tell me not to cross my bridges before coming to them. Yet in the event, in four years' time, the crisis of the Thirties had caught up with us and many of us had no teaching jobs to go to as we had been enjoined. It was another of those obligations or contracts where all the onus was on one side: you swore to teach but the Board of Education for their part, could not provide you with an opportunity to do so after spending four years in qualifying.

I found out that my first year's course would cause no difficulty, except that in Greek I would have to put in some real work; and possibly in Anglo-Saxon, as they used to call Old English in those days. I had not taken any Greek at school and I would have to reach approximately Higher Schools standard in one year. Fortunately, I took to the subject, and we had a good tutor in Kathleen Freeman who was a first-class Greek scholar. (She later made her name as a novelist and writer of detective stories under the name of Mary Fitt.) The head of the department was Professor Tillyard, a brother to E. M. W. Tillyard, the Cambridge Shakespearian scholar. The professor of Latin was also a Cambridge man, W. W. Grundy, who invariably used a Gladstone bag to carry his papers. It was hinted that the Gladstone was better suited for a non-academic purpose as it would carry a bottle of whisky much more unobtrusively than the usual brief-case. An abiding picture of him comes up, hurrying along the corridors to and from the lecture rooms with his bag full of papers, his head, with its bald crown and inexpertly trimmed fringe (I believe his wife used to operate on it), slightly forward. He was said to be an expert soccer player, a member of one of the two teams of his native Manchester. It was easy to imagine him as a younger man, tripping along the wing and deceiving the opposition by his slightly pigeon-toed gait. The titbit about his carrying whisky in his Gladstone may have been undergraduate slander; yet there may have been some truth in it judging from the conviction with which he rendered the passage from Horace when we were reading the *Epistles*:

Nulla placere diu nec vivere carmina possunt
Quae scribuntur aquae potoribus.

Poems do not please for long, nor yet shall live,
That are written by drinkers of water.

Leopold Richardson, an Irishman, later secretary of the Classical
Association, was senior lecturer in the Latin department before
becoming professor of Greek, successor to Tillyard. My earliest
memory of him was his proceeding through Cathays Park to the College
for a two o'clock lecture on the *Letters of the Younger Pliny* while a goodly
proportion of his prospective class were going in the opposite direction,
down to the Capitol Cinema. It was a Monday and one of the first
performances of that great novelty, the 'talking pictures'. Al Jolson and
Janet Gaynor were much more exciting to us at that time than the letters
of Pliny, even when they were describing the eruption of Vesuvius and
the death of his uncle. Later on in my final honours year when we had
Leopold Richardson as a tutor—there were just two pupils in this
group—he instilled in me a lasting love of the *Georgics* that I came to
consider a much better poem than Virgil's *Aeneid*, in spite of this poem's
near-worship by generations of scholars and readers. C. Day Lewis's
excellent translation of the *Georgics*, made during the last war, has
confirmed the quality of the poem and the conviction that the poet was
singing out of his own experience, singing his real self and his love for
the countryside and his enduring, fellow-feeling for the perennial work
of the farmer.

The history professor was a sick man who was just coming to the end
of his career. He attended when he could, and if there was an occasional
examination or written test, he sent his wife, an unsmiling dragon, to
invigilate. The department was virtually run at this time by Dr William
Rees who specialized in Welsh history. He was an excellent teacher,
positive and clear in his exposition. He was one of the few historians who
used maps extensively; and it was use of a map that got 'Doc' Rees
another nickname during our course. In medieval Welsh history he was
using a map that showed the 'commotes' or administrative divisions.
More than once, to refer to a commote in north Wales he placed his
hand over the particular division, spreading his fingers to make his point
emphatically, and mouthing its name, *Y Perfedd Wlad* (the Middle
Land). This action used to amuse two or three girls from the valleys and
thereafter they would refer to Doc Rees as *Diawl Y Perfedd Wlad* (the
Devil of Y Perfedd Wlad). Dr Rees carried the department through a
very difficult time. He was a first-class historian and later got a chair,
becoming widely known here and in the U.S.A.

Another of our teachers I came into contact with was Professor Brett of the English department. He was a regular attender at college 'Smokers', the concerts that were held annually at one of the big city hotels. The air at these concerts was invariably very thick, not only with smoke. But Professor Brett was broadminded and used to say that he didn't mind if the stories that were told, and the songs that were sung, were rabelaisian as long as they were witty and well put over. He was a short man who used to walk with a slow deliberate step; it was said that he had a heart condition. His egg-shaped head was covered with close cropped hair and he never wore a hat. He wore an old-fashioned jacket with high revers and a high stiff collar with a very narrow tie. He had a deep authoritative voice and his owl-like bespectacled face was always cheerful. His lectures on Chaucer were peppered with asides that made the hour fly. He was a Cambridge man and he gave us an interesting sidelight on the Cambridge master's gown he wore while lecturing. He demonstrated that the gown's long 'wings', that flapped about his short legs as he paced the lecture-room platform, were once used, in less expansive times, as pockets where the needy Masters of Arts would secrete crusts and titbits of food.

My playing for the college rugby team made more impact on me than the academic work, especially at first. The away matches were memorable for their exploring of new country. We played many of our matches in the Forest of Dean, Gloucester, Cheltenham and in what is called the West Country; and in the first team we seemed to be more often heading east rather than west, to Lydney, Bream, Cinderford and in some years Barnstaple, Bridgwater, Exeter. The usual pattern of these outings was to find a pub after the game, and the game would sometimes be played over again during the evening. We stopped more than once in a delightful old pub in Cheltenham. It seemed to us, over fifty years ago, not to have altered at all since the days when horses drew the only traffic on the roads. It was an old coaching inn and the walls were hung with sporting prints and a couple of coachman's horns. Its shelves were festooned with highly polished copper measures and pewter drinking mugs—the kind of inn one links with Surtees. The barmaid was a friendly person who gave us some homely but cryptic advice which I imagine she gave to the boys who had just started frequenting pubs: 'S.T.B., lads, S.T.B., then you won't go far wrong.' Returning by road from one of these outings we called at the farm of an uncle of Fred Weston's. He had just finished making cider, now stored in large barrels in a cellar. He invited us to go down and after indicating a barrel that had some mature cider, left us to help ourselves. It was one of the strongest drinks I had tasted and was very rightly included in the friendly barmaid's prohibition: STICK TO BEER, STICK TO BEER. Before we had been an hour in the coach on our way home most of the team were boisterous, fuddled, or dead asleep.

Two of the College team came from Ynysbwl and in the vacation I used to play with them in their team: they were Dafydd Aubrey Thomas and Claude Neath; and often out of term I walked over Gilfach-yr-Hydd hill to call on them and we would wander up to Llanwynno, tiring the sun with talk and occasionally stopping to watch a diversion, such as a farmer schooling a young sheep dog on the breast of the opposite hill. He had an older dog with him and he sent it after the half dozen sheep that were in the field, forcing the learner to watch him in spite of being eager to follow in the exciting game of rounding up the sheep. Dafydd Aubrey knew the history of the area and he would spice the walk lightly with remarks such as the one that the Mynachdy, a farm we had just passed, was a grange to Margam Abbey. Camden, the Elizabethan antiquary, had visited the Clydach valley and had seen the farm, which had ceased to be a monastic establishment earlier in the sixteenth century. Most of our talk was about more immediate concerns than this; about the coming games, and about personalities in the College. Dafydd was two or three years older than I and much better read. His father was a headmaster and county councillor and he profited from long discussions with him. On one of our walks Dafydd Aubrey told me about the Nottingham miner's son, D. H. Lawrence, whose name I was hearing for the first time. He had just been reading *The White Peacock* and praised the book highly, saying that it had been set in a place like Ynysbwl or any of the valley villages where the coal mines had been opened up not many years before in the middle of farming country, just like the scene we were then seeing.

But strangely enough I did not show much desire to read Lawrence. At this stage my life was so active that I had no time for reading except those books I had to read for the various courses. I had, for instance, read few novels except those that were on the various school syllabuses, novels by Scott, Dickens, George Eliot, Marryat and Kingsley. As far as English literature itself was concerned I had not awakened to it; literature for me at that time was like something in a glass case, preserved and enshrined: time the arbitrator had chosen it for veneration and we could not do anything about it. It was like a beautifully laid out garden that belonged to somebody else. When you noticed it you looked over the fence and admired it in passing. I was always passing at that stage. But Dafydd Aubrey—either because he was brought up in a different household or because his own life had a different rhythm—had grown up earlier. He was two years older and compared with him I was undeveloped, suffering from a protracted adolescence. He was reading French, philosophy and theology, and he had his career mapped out. His plan was to train as a medical missionary, and he was reading for an arts degree before switching over to six years' medical training. During my first year we travelled together between home and college and we were often together on rugby trips so that I got to know him well. Later in my second year he stayed in lodgings in Cardiff, a better centre for his journeys around the county on his Sunday preaching engagements. For all those who entered college as 'ministerials' preached regularly on a Sunday, during term time, in the various denominational chapels that were within striking distance of the College. It was a committed life, and the majority had little leisure for college social activities as they had to fit in their preaching and the preparation that it entailed with their degree work. Dafydd Aubrey was one of the few ministerials who played rugby, and was thus exposed to the temptations that most rugby players meet—to allay their after-the-match thirst by drinking a lot of beer.

Dafydd Aubrey inferred humorously that his grandfather, who had been a pit-sinker, had insinuated a fondness for beer into his father's genes where they had been dormant, and they had abundantly surfaced in his own. His natural delight in good fellowship and in the relaxed atmosphere of a pub, bothered him tremendously, especially when he preached on a Sunday following an away match, the night before having had a 'session' with the boys. He was the most sincere and compassionate man it had been my good fortune to meet, yet he was aware that his drinking, although a venial sin, was not so regarded by Y Duwiol (The Godly); and for that reason he was troubled in his own conscience; not in any absolute sense, I am sure, but for the sufficient reason that he was letting his well-wishers down—chiefly his own family. His conflict was acute in a way that it would be hard for us to imagine now; for drinking, especially open drinking in a public place, was then a sin against the Holy Ghost and deserved, as some of the 'unco guid' used to maintain, incarceration in the deepest and hottest pit of Hell. But the irony was that when Dafydd Aubrey had a few drinks it seemed his humane qualities would flower: he was the world's friend, the friend especially of the underprivileged. When he was lit up, his benevolence knew no bounds; it was as if he would seek to extend his feeling of the potential rightness of things indefinitely. He believed that if only we could reach rightness of thought in harness with right feelings it would be possible to attain a kind of revelation, where we should see not only the way out of our own personal difficulties but also a cure for the social injustice we were experiencing so acutely in the valleys.

It was a journey to Oxford that was the cause of the crisis in Dafydd Aubrey's life. We were playing rugby against Jesus College and we went up from Cardiff by road starting at eight o'clock. We reached Oxford in time for an early lunch. The lunch it was that began the day's proceedings, for with it we were served beer in two and three pint sconces—earthenware drinking vessels with two handles. Many of the colleges at that period brewed their own beer, and the Jesus beer was thick and very potent. Most of the team were well primed before the match; the tipplers of course included Dafydd Aubrey. We were allocated to the individual rooms of the college team to change into our football gear. I went to the rooms of a man named Pritchard who had been at Monmouth School. He was reading classics; and I envied him his comfortable quarters, with his textbooks all neat and orderly to hand. We had a good game which we won and then had tea in the junior common-room with a special Oxford delicacy, crumpets and a savoury paste. There was a piano in the common-room and one of the Cardiff boys started to experiment with it; and an Oxford man suggested a song, but the singing was almost muted as if weighted by the august tradition of 'Coleg Y Iesu'. Whatever it was the singing didn't get off the ground. Shortly afterwards we went to the Mitre, the famous Oxford hostelry—now converted into a mere eating house—and all inhibitions went out by the window. The main bar of the Mitre was divided into discreet, oaken cubicles, seating a party of four or perhaps six. As the evening went on our party got boisterous. Dafydd Aubrey was in his element; orating and reciting and getting to his feet and sitting down with such abandon that eventually the seat gave way with a crack that brought silence to a full room. In the meantime, two or three of the team had purloined a couple of bikes resting in an area at the back of the premises and were riding them recklessly around the small space while a waiter was vainly trying to restrain them. It was time to leave. When we got out we were met by two Cardiff men who were out of breath, having just escaped from the proctor's men. The journey home followed the usual pattern: at the start there was bedlam, followed by a boozy bout of singing which trailed as the beer wore off into comparative quiet. We got back to Cardiff well after midnight and two of us valley boys slept on the floor of Dafydd Aubrey's 'digs' where he stayed with the other students. He was too late getting up from his bed to keep his preaching engagement; and he never preached again as a ministerial.

Later in the year he left Cardiff for the University of Edinburgh to read medicine. Afterwards I saw him only during the vacations when we played football together, and occasionally we would walk over the hills and he would recount some of his adventures in Edinburgh. He had met an Englishman on his medical course who shared his predilection for beer and they became boon companions. One story he told me described his attending the Englishman's wedding in London. It was a fashionable wedding as the bridegroom's family was a titled one. They started from Edinburgh in a sports car and after an eventful odyssey reached London in time, and fairly sober. Dafydd Aubrey had borrowed a dress-suit for the occasion. He said: 'I almost looked the part except that I had to wear the trousers a bit low. The only socks I had with me were a pair of rugby ones.' Years later when we lived in Suffolk at Blaxhall, near Snape and Aldeburgh, he and his wife, Mair, came to visit us. After looking round it struck him that he had been in these parts before. He then remembered staying at Snape, the next village. He and his friend, Anthony Gathorne-Hardy, had arrived from Edinburgh with the boot of the car full of anatomical specimens. 'That was about twenty-five years ago. We stayed at The Priory with his mother.' His friend's mother was the Dowager Countess of Cranbrook, and it was typical of him not to mention his connections. Miner or nobleman, he was concerned with the man not the rank.

After the first year at Cardiff I no longer travelled to college by train. Buses started running from the surrounding valleys to the city, and they were cheaper and more frequent. The Aberdare buses from our valley dropped us conveniently just outside the college so that it was possible to get to a nine o'clock lecture by leaving home just an hour before. Owing to the frequency of the buses I spent little time at home during term, travelling in on an early bus and returning at ten or eleven o'clock. Although I slept at home I had distanced myself to a large extent from the family. My interests were now centred in the college, in sport, new friends, and the social life. I became friendly with and flirted around with one or two girls I used to meet in the Students' Union where a great deal of my time was wasted. There was a dining-room and lounge there, and a billiard table in what had been the drawing-room of a fairly large private house; and it was easy to pick out from the people who attended the Union a group who were only half-hearted about their academic studies, though some of the regulars frittered a great deal of time during term but worked furiously during the vacations to make up for it. My second year was theoretically an easy one as I had no examination in Latin, my main subject. My chief effort went into Greek. We were reading Euripides and Plato and I was enjoying both the play and the trial and death of Socrates, but learning the language as opposed to a mere translation of the texts needed real application; but I was doing enough work to pass the examinations. Often as I travelled home on a late bus—even after working in the library—I felt dissatisfied with myself as I knew vaguely that I was not getting to grips with my work for its own sake: I was aiming simply to slip by the examiners. I was aware that I was only working at half-power and in fact doing a botched job. But when I looked at the alternative what was I to do? I had developed this pattern of not aiming at excellence during the disturbed time at the latter end of my school career, and it was too late to start now. Were the difficulties at home—to put it bluntly—an excuse for laziness and not the real cause? After these periods of introspection I usually gave up trying to solve my own problems and fell back on living-for-the-moment. Yet I determined to stiffen myself up to do enough work to get a degree, if not yet of the highest class, still not of the lowest.

The examination went well and it was a halcyon summer; and when the vacation started I began practising sprinting. For a week or so I had a temporary post doing my old job. The Co-operative delivery man was off work and my father suggested to the manager that I would stand in for him. It was a welcome break, and I looked forward to doing some of my old work again, though the chief attraction was the pay at the end of the week. The horse was a lightish Shire cross-bred, or possibly a Clydesdale, and was much bigger than the fourteen and a half hands of our Welsh cob, Dick. After being three years away from delivering goods I was surprised at how much I enjoyed the work. The horse, though a bit unwieldy at first, was quite placid; and I knew the round as I had covered it so many times before. It was the same and yet it was different. On this job I now had a definite and limited responsibility: as long as I delivered the goods to the satisfaction of the customers, that was all that was expected of me. There was nothing in the background to worry about. I didn't pack the goods; and I was not concerned with the business, with wondering how it was going and how long it was likely to last. I finished the day's job, bedded the horse and went home in the evening and forgot about everything. The work was in fact lighter: I carted few heavy sacks, none of the heavy sacks of meal and flour I used to take up to the farms. Instead, it was chiefly groceries and occasionally a half hundredweight of chicken feed. When I went up to my old haunts up on the Graig away out of the village I let the horse go at his own leisurely pace, making the trip last longer like a real carter. On one of my deliveries that week I took the groceries into the living-room of a cottage where I heard my first electric-mains wireless, as it was called then. There was a snatch of Henry Hall's music, among the first of a succession of dance bands playing between five and six o'clock on the BBC, booming out of a moving-coil speaker; and I was much impressed. I could almost envy the rhythm of a routine job during the day, after which I could relax in the evening not giving it a thought until the morrow.

Very shortly after getting to college I got to know W. J. A. (Bill) Evans from Pontypridd. His father was a Welsh Methodist minister who had died when Bill was very young; and his mother kept a bootshop in the town. He played rugby and was a member of the college boxing team; and he became one of the leading lights of the group from the valleys who played games and went about together. A few of us had arranged to go on a camping holiday towards the end of the summer near Porthcawl on the Glamorgan coast.

We pitched our tent on its own, less than a hundred yards from the sea—the restless ever-moiling sea that, apart from a thunderstorm, was a placid well behaved pond for the whole of the time we were there, the tide slowly coming up the channel and discreetly receding day after day making only the faintest of murmurs in its movement. This part of the coast could be very rough, but for three weeks it was as calm as a judge with only a thunderstorm to point the contrast and to remind us of our good fortune. The sun rose and shone dutifully day after day, sinking at night in a vivid red glow. Then a soft twilight with the shore lights appearing on the other side of the channel, the signalling of the lighthouses heralding the evening when we would walk into the neighbouring town looking for adventure. There were four of us: Bill Evans, Claude Neath, Walter Gomer Rees and myself. Gomer and Claude were miners' sons and none of us had more than a minimum of cash for a holiday but we were determined to stay on the coast as long as we could. In spite of our money soon running out we continued to live on shell-fish, failing to catch any of the rabbits on the dunes. Bill volunteered to sell his camera so that we were able to last out the three weeks. We had little money to spend, so we lazed about in the sun for most of the day, only broken by periods of intense effort when, to save going a long distance for water, we dug a well in the sand, getting a tea chest from an old lady who kept a shop in the village of Newton. When we knocked out its bottom and sank it in the hole we had dug, it collected enough water to serve our needs. The rest of the time we spent in bathing and listening to the gramophone belonging to three girls who had a tent on a dune not far from ours. About half-past six we cooked a meal on the primus stove; and then we cleaned ourselves up and walked into Porthcawl for the 'night life'. This meant strolling along the esplanade seeing who was there and 'getting off' if we could, with any likely girls who were themselves out prospecting. Along the front we passed the boarding houses and the expensive hotels that served 'dinner with the blinds up', just as I observed later in Cambridge. The correct diners in their dress-suits, like fish in an aquarium, were swimming in the consciousness of being noticed by the visitors who passed along the promenade outside. Alternatively, we visited a pub, had a drink or two and then went to the pavilion near the beach where there was a band, and spent the evening dancing.

The memory remains of this as of a life on another plane. I had three good companions and a cross word was never spoken all the time we were in camp; three weeks of simple, innocent enjoyment. We were twenty years of age and really *innocent*. Our poverty made us so. We couldn't drink more than a pint or two of beer because we hadn't the money. We talked knowledgeably about girls but I feel sure that none of us had lain with a girl in the old-fashioned meaning of the phrase. We heard stories about 'nancy' boys or 'dilly' boys, the current slang for homosexuals; but we considered them as *yarns*, dirty stories. We did not believe homosexuality existed. The backwash of the Oscar Wilde case still lapped about male conversation and his name figured in common-room verses like *The Ballad of the Good Ship Venus*, but we did not give actual credence to it. It was not until three or four years later that we were really enlightened. Claude Neath got a job in one of the lesser-known public schools. After he had been there about a year there was an outbreak of homosexual behaviour among the boys who were boarders. The headmaster was worried, and immediately consulted the head of a nearby boarding school. He came back relieved if not absolutely reassured. The message in effect was: 'Don't worry too much. As a matter of fact it is rife.'

There was one facet of my life that continually bothered my conscience. This was the selfishness, the heart-hardening that I put between myself and the struggle of the family, and the distress that was patent in the valleys. Fortunately unemployment was not as bad in my home of Abercynon. The colliery, owned by Guest, Keen and Nettlefold, was a large and productive one and appeared to keep its complement of men for much of this period. But higher up the Merthyr valley, where the Prince of Wales made a much-publicized visit a few years later, over two-thirds of the working population were without jobs, and many had been idle for nine or ten years. I was aware of the distress but did not feel it; it was not happening to me and, deep down, in spite of my intellectual awareness I did not *know* it. It was some time before I became conscious of what was happening outside my own preoccupations and was finally able to pull my head out of the sand.

In one sense I enjoyed this last year of my degree in that I worked more, and my conscience troubled me the less for that reason. Although I ploughed laboriously through a great deal of the work that was on the syllabus—particularly on the language side and the construction of Latin prose—I enjoyed reading the texts and the discussion of Roman literature. In this process I laid the foundation for a permanent attachment to Catullus, Virgil and Horace, and Livy, Cicero and Tacitus among the prose writers.

In the examination I got what I expected: a second-class honours in the second division. There were no 'firsts' in the university that year. Considering that I had not worked hard enough in my first two years it was a just result. Then came my year of professional training. The school where I did the bulk of it was in Cardiff. It was a Roman Catholic secondary school run by an order of Christian Brothers, celibates who lived in a hostel nearby. As soon as I entered this school I reacted against it as though by instinct: the sickly-sweet image of the Virgin Mary with a light burning beside it hung on the wall of the corridor and I was involuntarily repelled. I did not know why.

I reported to the headmaster Brother Gilbert who wore a soutane as did all the brothers, except one or two laymen on the staff who wore gowns. Brother Gilbert also wore steel-rimmed glasses. He was courteous and clinically correct. He introduced me to the first-form Brother whose class I was to take in Latin. He also supervised some sixth-formers who were studying for the priesthood and were taking Greek, in which I was scheduled to assist. I liked the students, who were chiefly Irish, but failed to make contact with any of the staff. One of my first surprises was that I and the science man, who was a student with me, were not allowed in the staff-room. I was surprised because I knew that my friends in the valley schools were all on easy terms with the staff and used their room freely. Here, a classroom was pointed out to us and it was suggested that we should eat the sandwiches we had brought for lunch in there at two of the desks. Our contact with the staff was minimal and clearly we were only there on sufferance, probably conceded by the school in return for a grant made by the City Education Committee towards its upkeep. While I was there the only man I had a conversation with—lasting more than a few sentences—was the caretaker, a soft-spoken Irishman. He had served his apprenticeship as a cleaner at University College.

I had been a fortnight in the school when I was visited by my education tutor, Evan John as we called him—E. J. Jones—who came from the valleys and spoke our language. He told me in a friendly way that Brother Gilbert found my mode of dress was not exactly right for the school and he advised me to change it. I wore, as many students did then, a pair of flannel trousers, a pullover and a sports jacket. He wanted to see me in a correct dark suit. Fortunately I had a darkish suit, not exactly Sunday black; but I resented using it for everyday wear as it was probable that it would have to last me a long time: I did not know when I would get another. I have often wondered since whether if circumstances had been different and I had found my first school amenable I would have overcome my prejudice to a teaching career. I very much doubt it. In any case, the friendly schools were few and far between and were only given their tone by a headmaster who had qualities other than those of a competent, even outstanding, administrator. Yet it has occurred to me since that there was a great deal of anti-Catholic feeling in south Wales fifty and sixty years ago. I had heard our minister refer in more than one of his sermons to 'Yr Hen Bab' (the Old Pope) in a disparaging way. I remember, too, the building of a Catholic church in our village just after the First World War on a site between the canal and the river. Most of the people of Abercynon were not disturbed by this. But when the priest discovered that a trickle of water that ran conveniently into the river near the church was, in fact, a holy well opinion hardened against them; and people looked with some cynicism at the charabancs full of worshippers arriving to bathe various parts of their bodies in the spring, and to take bottles of holy water away with them. Relations between Protestants and Catholics have improved considerably since then. When I raised my lack of sympathy with the Christian brothers, as they were a half century ago, with a Catholic friend who had himself taught in one of their establishments in Ireland he hinted that within his experience of fifteen years earlier they had a limited and rather illiberal outlook.

I was reminded of the building of the Abercynon Catholic Church quite recently by a strange coincidence. Early one fine August morning four or five years ago when I or my wife went out to fetch the milk we saw an oldish man sitting on the grass bank by the side of the road just outside our cottage in Brooke, Norfolk. He had obviously spent the night out. Exactly where he spent it I learned later; it was in a barn near the Bungay road on the south side of our village, confirming, incidentally, the old East Anglian saying: 'In a village, if you wait long enough you'll know everything.' He was probably tramping round doing seasonal work in the region. I went out to speak to him and after he had a cup of tea and something to eat I found out that he was a Glasgow Irishman who had been about the country a great deal. He knew from my accent that I was a Welshman, and when I told him where I was born he said: 'I know that place well. I built the stonework around the spring they had there—for Father Joseph who was the first priest that was in that church.' After he left us he spent the rest of the morning in the pub about a hundred yards down the road from our cottage.

We were in the schools for the first two days of the week; the other days were in college attending lectures in psychology, the history of education and the optional subjects that would prove extra strings to a prospective teacher. I chose handicrafts and an intensive course in physical training. In theory we were kept very busy but in a sense it was 'busyness' in a practical way: only occasionally were we called upon to write an essay where we had to do some real thinking. Undoubtedly much of the instruction was otiose in that you could not learn to teach by being told what to do: you had to get in the water and learn to swim yourself.

At the beginning of this session my younger brother, Sydney, had entered college on the science side. The science students seemed to work much harder than we did. They had long extended hours of laboratory work that appeared to take up most of their day. They attended regularly for nine o'clock lectures and left off at five o'clock. My brother and I rarely saw one another on the buses or in college, and we could have been living in different houses. I got into lectures later than he did and returned later at night. I then assumed I should soon be away from home, and that would help to ease the pressure. I had begun applying for jobs at the end of the second term with the expectation of getting a post teaching my subject along with games. The members of my department in the previous year had all got posts during the previous two years, straight after qualifying, and my hope of getting one fairly soon seemed justified. The truth was that preoccupied with my own concerns—naive and apolitical as they were—I had not read the signs. The then government, the second Labour government, under Ramsay Macdonald, Philip Snowden and J. H. Thomas, was already in disarray in the face of the acute economic recession. But I was only dimly aware of this. I rarely read the front page of a newspaper and inhabited a tight, almost solipsist world. If I read it at all, it was only the sports page. I had started to apply for a teaching post at the end of the second term and I continued to scour the columns of *The Times Educational Supplement* every week. But I was not unduly alarmed by the apparent shortage of jobs in my subject: so great was my confidence—in spite of my lack of enthusiasm for teaching—that I would somehow get a post.

Abercynon Colliery

Abercynon

# 6 · Crisis

It was July 1931. I had finished my university career, such as it was, and I was now entering a bleak and black period of my life, though I did not know it at the time. It was over three years before I got a regular job—which was partly my own fault because I was divided in my aim. Yet this period enabled me ultimately to find my own purpose in life and gave me the centre that I lacked. Up to the end of the first year after my leaving the university I was a drifter, not sure of what I wanted to do. It was only then that I grew up, and knew in my bones what direction my life should take. It is for this reason that I have since thought that after leaving school a young person should not proceed to university straight away but should have a break of at least a year when he should do something else—get out of the academic mould and experience life from an entirely different angle. He should escape, at least temporarily, from the narrow confines of books and become acquainted with that part of existence where the supreme educator is not texts but experience. I am aware that I am arguing from my own feelings and I am conscious that others may think differently, yet I am sure that many young people suffer from a prolonged adolescence, as I myself did, through being immured in the academic corridors until they are well into their twenties; and the rites of passage to another stage of their life become correspondingly more painful.

On leaving university, I was insulated from almost everything beyond my own personal concerns and I blithely expected to get a post as a matter of course. I did not have a brilliant degree but it was 'middle of the road' and it was supported by involvement in college games. But nothing happened: all my applications for a post came to nothing and I began to get concerned. Now, too, the newspapers were full of the impending financial crisis. The second Labour government was beginning to break up. Earlier in the year Oswald Mosley as a member of the government had proposed a scheme involving an extension of pensions and a big programme of public works to absorb the massive army of unemployed. It was rejected and he left the government to form a new party. Now on 23 August the Labour government was forced into the invidious measure of proposing a cut of ten per cent at the expense of the unemployed. It was debated in Cabinet and its members split on this issue. The next day Ramsay Macdonald, Philip Snowden, J. H. Thomas and Lord Sankey combined with the Conservatives and Liberals to form the first National Government. At this stage even I began to take interest in what was happening. The papers were thick with J. H. Thomas's pronouncements: he was finance minister and was responsible for steering the government out of the crisis. Although I was still in the political kindergarten his reported statements struck me as weak and futile. I remember particularly his utterance: 'We shall explore every avenue' as being a fair example of their vague powerlessness to tackle the disaster. The columnist Beachcomber now took up this sentence and made derisive and cruel play of his image of exploring every avenue. Unfortunately, Jimmy Thomas, like many south Walians, was not too sure of his aitches. This gave the phrase a slightly comic twist, and the humorists made hay with it.

During this time I spent many hours with Claude Neath. We were both without jobs and this naturally drew us together. As soon as the football season started we met regularly. We often met on the hill that divided our valleys, discussing tactics for applying for jobs and silently commiserating with one another. The prospect was not exhilarating. The National Government began to lay about them without delay: ten per cent cut in the unemployed benefits and the pay of all public employees: civil service, teachers, police, post office and the armed forces—the last causing a mutiny of the Atlantic Fleet at Invergordon just as they were about to leave for their autumn exercises. We were well and truly in the mire now. Cuts and retrenchments were instantly made in both state and private schools. There was a particular shortage in classics jobs as it appeared that in the current economics the classics were the first to suffer. It could be said that this retrenchment was the beginning of the long decline in the teaching of Latin and Greek in state grammar schools. In this climate, Claude and I discussed the chances of getting posts as objectively as we could. One thing we were certain of: we should hang on, applying for posts only in our own subjects. Otherwise—and this applied to me more than to Claude—once we took up an appointment teaching some other subject it would be extremely difficult to switch back to teaching classics. Especially was this so as the position was likely to worsen and fewer jobs would be going.

We continued to walk about the countryside, playing football at week-ends. One regular walk was to Pontypridd, the nearest town, where we spent an hour or so in the reading-room of the library conning the educational papers for vacant posts. After that we spent an hour in a pub nursing a half-pint of beer we walked home. A few weeks before Christmas, Claude got a temporary post at Preston in Lancashire. A master in a boarding school was taken ill and he took his place for the rest of the term. He had a better degree than I had for the reason that he had spent an extra year taking honours in Greek as well as Latin. I was glad for his sake, but now I was on my own and I felt my position acutely.

I had no replies or merely a bare acknowledgement from the applications I had made and began to feel less and less hopeful though on the surface I tried to put up an impassive front. I walked to Pontypridd regularly, meeting one or two graduates who were still out of work and spending an hour or so combing the educational papers for likely posts. During the day I spent a great deal of time reading whatever I could get hold of. In the evenings I walked the roads about the valleys, often going up to Nelson, a nearby village where my eldest sister now lived. Dinah and her husband Jack Bickham had recently started a family; and as he worked by night at Treharris colliery he was often free for a talk during the afternoon or early evening. It was usually about his job at the bottom of the pit shaft where as a 'hitcher' he loaded the trams of coal into the cage to be hauled to the surface. When the cage came down he had to hitch the empty trams on to a 'journey' ready to be hauled back to the coal face to be distributed to the colliers in their working places or stalls. As a hitcher he knew a great deal of what was going on in the pit; everybody who came down the shaft would pass the hitchers to get to the workings. It was absorbing to listen to his description of the various personalities and incidents that happened during the day in the colliery. I spent a lot of time with Dinah and Jack at this time. They had a wireless which was a great attraction. Jack had built it himself; at first a crystal set with headphones and later a set with valves and a loudspeaker.

Christmas came and went. Claude got a boarding-school post in the Cotswolds on the strength of his experience in the Lancashire school. For me the waiting for a grammar school appointment had not paid off. I now decided to apply for schools irrespective of their grade. But even jobs in elementary schools were difficult to get in the middle of the school year and the few applications I made had no success. By Easter I became desperate; and I decided to go up to London to register as a supply teacher with the London County Council. This was scraping the bottom of the barrel and was comically other than my sanguine expectations when I trained in my final year. When I qualified I had even gone to the trouble of finding out the salary of a secondary or grammar school teacher. It was £230 a year, a princely sum that helped to allay my doubts about taking up a career I was committed to but was entering without enthusiasm. Supply teaching was irregular work, you were paid like a journeyman on piece-work, by the day, and there was no pay for school holidays.

In the meantime my brother Sydney had been to Maesteg to stay with our uncle, Will Hitchings, and his sister Averina. Will bred horses and it was a holiday for Syd. While he was there Will taught him the skill of repairing boots and when he came home Syd passed the skill on to me. I now repaired my own shoes that by this time, owing to the amount of walking I had been doing, were nearly off my feet. I had a jacket but I needed a pair of trousers before I made the journey to London. At this point I approached my sister Esme. She was a nurse in a Cardiff hospital and lent me £3 that enabled me to buy a pair of cheap flannels and covered my fare up to London. Two of my younger brothers were already up in London: Ken was working in an office, Roy in a factory. Ken was lodging in Shepherd's Bush and I arranged to stay the night with him on my arrival. This was the second time I was in the city. On my first visit to the Empire Exhibition at Wembley I was taken in by the glamour of London seen through the eyes of a schoolboy. This time, although the schoolboy was a little older, he still had a callow streak and was just beginning his real education. I had, nevertheless, a plan of campaign. This was to contact the Greenwich Division of the L.C.C. where I had previously applied for a job and where I was told I would be tolerably certain of getting supply work. I went up by bus as it was much cheaper than the train. I travelled on a Sunday on a leisurely ride through the Cotswolds and through Witney and Oxford. I found my brother Ken, stayed with him the night and on the Monday morning made for

Greenwich. Luck was with me. The secretary at Greenwich told me there was a supply job going at a school at Peckham Rye not far away. I went straight to the school and was interviewed by the headmaster. He was an old soldier and I got on well with him. He told me, when I got to know him better, that there were two sorts of Welshman—the good and the bad. He gave me the benefit of the doubt; the other sort, he said, the 'line-shooters', often peddled an atrocious line of blarney. I explained that I had just come up from Wales and I had not yet got anywhere to stay. He immediately got on the telephone to the landlady where one of his staff had formerly lived. He told me that she would take me; and my immediate difficulties were over.

During this stay in London I sampled two of the usual diversions of a Thirties valley boy going up to London for what was effectively the first time. These were a visit to one of the Welsh chapels and a Sunday evening experience at Marble Arch, where the Welsh used to gather in a fair-sized crowd. It was a good place to renew acquaintances, and in the short time I was there I met two or three people I knew in the valleys. Many came up to the Welsh corner simply to sing and as it was a Sunday night most of the singing was of Welsh hymns. But I had temporarily lost my *hwyl* for singing and left fairly early for my long bus ride to East Dulwich. With Ken I also visited the Welsh Chapel at Castle Street, near Upper Regent Street. But our visit was not a comfortable one. We both wore flannels, out of necessity not choice, while the rest of the congregation were in conventional Bible black. But by this time I was growing a thicker skin and ignored the looks of the regulars, the properly attired faithful.

The end of term finally came and I made for Paddington Station as soon as school closed. The six o'clock train was packed full of teachers from south Wales going home for the holidays. I saw many faces I recognized, but I had arranged to travel down with Bill Evans who had come from Cambridge and had managed to get across from Liverpool street to catch this train.

There was a kind of intuition pricking at the back of my mind as I travelled down from Paddington. If the feeling had expressed itself in words it would have said to me: 'Are you wise to go home like this, just for the prospect of a couple of weeks' camping with the boys?' It would have been better to stay in London. I still had no permanent job and although there would be no teaching jobs as the schools would be closed until the autumn, I could look around for any kind of work. I dismissed the idea almost as soon as it occurred to me. Yet I was not happy about leaving the city. But I brushed aside the inward objection. It was one of the few occasions when I ignored my instinct, the faint voice, and I regretted it before many weeks were out. It was, however, enough to fix the truth in my mind ὑπήκουσα τῳ δαιμονίῳ (listen to your daimon). The command was plain enough and I paid for not listening to it. Going back to Wales cost me months of misery and indecision, of walking on the hills trying to decide what to do and getting into a state of panic at my failure to get a post. The fix I was in perpetually, with no one to discuss it with me, turned inevitably to apathy. Then I became alarmed when I was able to stand aside and see the position I was really in. I told no one of my real plight out of a silly pride, and my mind was a grey turmoil. Every attempt I made to escape from the morass seemed to suck me further in. I walked once a week the four miles to Pontypridd to see the educational papers. I was looking for a magical deliverance but it never came. I saw my friends in the school holidays, but I was ashamed at my failure and began to avoid them.

During those weeks I reached the bottom, although I tried to put a good face on my real state. I did a fair amount of coaching and got a bare subsistence which salved my conscience by paying for my keep. There was of course no unemployment pay as I had never contributed, having no insurance card. I had at this time one regular task: keeping the family's footwear in repair. I was skilled enough by now to resole a pair of boots or shoes by stitching the new soles on to the uppers. I would buy a bend of leather in Pontypridd, a length measuring about three and a half feet by two. It was enough to keep me going for a while; and I found repairing shoes an enjoyable pastime. Having learned the basic skills and got into the rhythm, it was satisfying to do a job where the mind was free to think its own thoughts and at the same time to see the job shaping up gradually. It demanded a minimum application except in those occasional stages in the process that needed your full attention. I can well imagine the old village cobblers gaining a reputation as thinkers.

There was something about the slow process of shaping leather that seemed to induce thought. I found, for instance, that I could think more clearly and sensibly about my own position. I now blamed myself for it chiefly, for being high-minded and refusing at first to take *any* teaching job I could get. But I was really unrepentant deep down, even though I was suffering for it now. Yet I was aware what was happening. It was not entirely personal: there were a couple of million like me; and the social and political side of unemployment forced themselves upon my mind.

Surely, unemployment in the twentieth century should not be treated like a natural disaster, like an act of God, like an earthquake that was beyond the scope of human responsibility. To infer that unemployment was inescapable was a betrayal of the hard-won and inbuilt responsibility of man to solve his own problems. Our ancestors had shown their ingenuity by inventing the wonderful machines that made the Industrial Revolution possible and had cleared the ground on which to build a second industrial edifice that would make their first groping discoveries look puny. Yet men, through their governments, had not been able to grapple with the basic human problem of our time: of want in plenty. They had failed to use the resources of the earth to their best advantage, directing the fruits to all, especially to the less favoured people wherever they may be.

One thing that my enforced idleness had succeeded in doing was to dragoon me into thinking for myself. As I repaired the boots and shoes, I was stimulated by an absorbing task that left the questing mind essentially free. Yet my thinking had been developed only to a point where it could barely be formulated, let alone acted upon. Nevertheless, as I polished off the welt of a pair of boots with a waxing iron, I could well echo the thoughts of generations of contemplative cobblers: 'Ah well, we can't solve the problems of the world but still we can mend old shoes.' Yet wry thoughts like these could not make me forget that my plight was as serious as I could imagine. I had reached a dead end and could not think of a way out. I plotted out the graph of my feeling throughout the past eighteen months: first the confidence that I could get a job when I completed my training; then mild surprise at the collapse of the labour market at the very time that I qualified; then the wistful thought that it was only temporary; and finally the growing conviction that the Depression was here to last. I was only vaguely aware that amid all these doubts and self-communings a revolution had happened within myself. Previously, I had been a real extrovert. My pleasures and my problems were plenty during my youth but they were nearly all outside me, or, at least, I identified them as having their origin in my circumstances and not in myself. Now I became morbidly introspective: all my thoughts were turned inward, and I spent endless hours as I walked about trying to think my way out, trying, as it were, to raise myself up by my own buskins. One evening while walking the road from one village to the next, I crossed a common and looked up at the remote sky with a faint moon and wisps of cloud scudding across it forlornly. I stopped and asked myself in despair: 'How long, O Lord, how long?' I was surprised at the utterance. I had not been to chapel for over a year, and as far as I had examined myself chapel seemed to me irrelevant. This was part of the revolution that had happened to me. Everything that had satisfied me in my life had been stripped away in recent months. I had ceased even to play football and had given up sprinting and had lost my friends, mainly through absence.

Shortly after this I met the local policeman, who suggested that I should join the police force. It was about as unlikely a job as I could imagine, but by this time I was convinced that I must try anything.

The following day I travelled to Cardiff. I timed my visit to the Chief Constable to catch him after he returned from lunch. The sergeant in charge gave me a seat after I had explained that I wanted to see the chief. Colonel Lindsay I knew as a 'bogey' in the valleys, the arch-enemy of the miners, organizer of protective posses of police who accompanied the 'blacklegs' or strike-breakers to work. As I was conjuring up a picture of the man as a big, bluff military figure—probably a bit of a bully—the man himself came in. The sergeant nodded and I got to my feet. He was a brisk, well dressed figure in civilian clothes, below average height and carrying his hat and a walking stick, more like a city club man than a chief constable. I approached him with my request to join the police force and he listened politely and asked me why I wanted to become a policeman. I told him I was a graduate but was out of a job. He paused at this and appeared to demur as he looked me over: 'Quite so, but it's muscle we want. Anyhow, the sergeant will take your measurements, and we'll see,' and he passed through to his office. The sergeant took me to a big room that I recognized as a tailor's cutting-room though there was no one on the bench at the time. He handed me over to one of the tailors who first weighed me and then measured me as though for a suit; 'I'll take your measurements just in case.' And in quarter of an hour I was out of the building having seen through the device immediately. Although I was asked my name and address I did not expect to hear anything. The measurement device was a part of the refusal, a protective ploy against the dozens of unsuitable applicants for entry to a force that already had a full complement.

As I expected I heard nothing more of the interview yet it had suggested a possible new opening, and when I saw an advertisement in one of the newspapers inviting applications to join the Palestine police I agonized for days over the question of whether I should apply or not. Eventually I decided that however badly I wanted a job I was not fitted to take up a career as a policeman. Later I thanked my daimon for preventing me going any farther with the idea. But there was one outcome of this attempt; it did force me to come out from the insidious apathy and inertia that long-term unemployment inevitably induces. At first came the irritation, the loss to one's self-esteem; then later came the withdrawal with the realization that, however you looked at it, fundamentally society did not want you: it had shunted you into a siding ready for the scrap-heap. The terrible thing is that at first you concur out of the listlessness that creeps over you on accepting this dismissive verdict. Unemployment eats into you like a cancer and I could feel myself slipping. Now, however, I started to fight back and consciously took myself in hand. I gave up smoking and had a glass of beer only occasionally when I was sure I could afford it. I lived like a monk and worked out my own course of rehabilitation. One of my first steps was to get myself fit again. I started in the winter and took to stripping to take long runs in the evenings, two or three miles along an unfrequented road. Alongside the physical programme, I started on an intense course of reading that Syd helped by bringing home books from the Cardiff library. One of the books I remember reading at this time was a thick digest of Gibbon's *Decline and Fall* which took me about a month to go through. I also discovered the *Sunday Referee*, a weekly paper owned by Isidore Ostrer. It had a section given over to young poets and writers. The editor of this feature was Victor Neuberg who published the early poems of Dylan Thomas and his friend Pamela Hansford Johnson. Bertrand Russell and C. E. M. Joad were among the writers who contributed to its literary pages, and there was a writer who called himself Vanoc II (W. Hayter Preston) who wrote a stimulating weekly column on contemporary topics. The appearance of the *Referee* once a week was to me like a bright light in a gloomy world. I was immensely interested in the lively articles: I got from them a cultural lifeline that I badly needed. In the literary section a number of prizes were given for verse translation of short poems in modern languages. There were also poems in Latin appearing about once a fortnight. I began competing, and to my surprise, a version of Horace's *Persicos odi, puer, apparatus*—I believe it was—appeared over my name and was followed by a small but useful prize, invaluable for me, in spite of its amount, for its emollient effect on my battered ego.

This was the break I had been waiting for; and it also made me aware of my neglect, while I was at college, of one of the delights I had at school, of writing for Alys Evans, the history mistress, a careful essay and being proud of the result. In college I wrote the prescribed essays in history as a chore. My heart was not in the effort. Now, however, I recaptured my delight in playing with words and it helped to give me back my self-respect. About then an advertisement appeared in a Cardiff newspaper inviting applications for the job of palaeographer at the Cardiff Library. I wrote to Leopold Richardson, who by this time had the chair of Greek, asking him whether I could use his name as a referee when I submitted my application. I had a letter by return of post; he remembered me in his Virgil class, offered to support my application and also told me of a class in palaeography that was just beginning at University College. But his postscript to the note was like a draught of cool water to someone who had been travelling across an arid desert. He wrote: 'I saw with pleasure your recent translations in the *Sunday Referee*.' I was overjoyed and took the note to the only place in the house where I could re-read it in privacy. It is not too much to say that the recognition of my small success, insignificant it itself, was my salvation. It was a token that a new way had opened. Up to then I had been groping blindly. Now I had found a path, an extremely rugged one, but one that my inner monitor applauded. I did not care ultimately what kind of job I took. I determined that my real work henceforth would be to write and I would go through hell, and farther, to follow it. Something had been happening ever since my interview with the chief constable. It was as though he was an unknowing catalyst to an underground interaction that had developed. It revealed itself like something I had noticed in my frequent walking on the hills. After a long winter, suddenly a strong growth of a small involuted green leaf of bracken would burst through the browning-red decay of the previous years and stand erect as the herald of a new spring. A pocket of cyclothymic energy had been storing up: now the pressure had reached its climax. It was like a mountain stream that had come against an obstacle that the autumn storms had blown across its path. The fallen tree with its massive bole, thick branches and accumulated detritus from the stream's daily flowing, had effectively built up a dam and left only a trickle of water to flow beyond the obstruction. Now the dam had suddenly burst under the pressure, and an unstoppable flow had shifted the tree and had carried away the rubbish in a turbid flood.

Plans and new ideas began to stir. I first started on an article that had been in my mind for months. Having no typewriter, it remained in manuscript. I then made up my mind to begin a project that came fresh to mind. In my final degree year I had read Plautus' *Captivi*—the play that exploits mistaken identity as its main theme. I liked the play and the idea came to me to reconstruct it as a radio play for children. Derek McCulloch and May Jenkin were broadcasting some very fine productions then and greatly enhancing the B.B.C.'s image with *Children's Hour*. Plautus' treatment of the plot of the mistaken identity had sparked me off and it did not really bother me that Shakespeare had used it before. In the meantime, my attempt was worth the trouble in that I learned my first lesson as a writer. If you have the germ of an idea and nothing comes, keep sitting as though your pants are glued to the chair until you have started to write and got some intelligible marks on the paper: *D'oes dim ond eisieu dechreu* (You have only to begin). Starting that mad project came to nothing. But I had gained a moral victory. Within a few days I had completed the draft of the play, and had stumbled across another lesson relevant to all writing: if the will is there, nothing will stop you. Although I realized that the play would be difficult to place, that was not important; I had finished the experiment I had set out to do. I had, most important of all, found my true purpose; and though it was a banal, Samuel Smiles truth I had experienced, I had experienced it myself. It worked, and now I could go on writing with the inner surety that ultimately I would succeed.

River Cynon

Abercynon

# 7 · Out of Work

At this time I had a full life except that I was earning a mere pittance. The writing was going on in spate and I was still keeping on with the coaching of a young law student in Ynysybwl, crossing the mountain three times a week. As the summer of 1934 went on, I continued furiously with the writing and the coaching, taking an occasional break, as I did for the meeting of unemployed miners I went to with Harry Jeffreys, my neighbour. The meeting was in Treharris and one of the speakers was S. O. Davies, the new Member of Parliament for Merthyr Tudful where most of the people were out of work. When Edward VIII visited the town a few years later, he saw the true state of a sizeable part of his nation and was appalled. The main speaker at Treharris was Wal Hannington, a Londoner, who was attempting to bring the number of the unemployed actively to the notice of the rest of the country. Statistics could be forgotten or ignored but marches and meetings were a constant reminder of the true position.

Another of the speakers was Mrs Despard, a remarkable old lady in an audience of unemployed miners. She was the sister of a British general of the First World War, a tall, gentle white-haired old lady who was in direct contrast to Wal Hannington who had, from the nature of his task, to be very decided and militant, not to say tough. She had been working among the unemployed in London and she made a deep impression on her present audience. It was the first meeting of miners I had been to for some years and I was struck by their seriousness. I was much more serious myself than I had been. Previously, I had gone to meetings at the Workmen's Hall in my own village more as a spectacle than anything else. Now I was involved as much as anyone there. I cannot remember much about the speeches yet I recall the intense concentration of the audience, especially when Wal Hannington was on his feet. Hanging on his lips was more than a cliché metaphor; they were picking the words out of his mouth.

As I walked home with Harry Jeffreys, I made up my mind to leave the valley. I would have another try at London. I had undertaken to coach my student for another few weeks until his examination and then I should be away. I had no real expectations for a play I had written about Warren Hastings; but some of the smaller, less ambitious manuscripts might find success. I would have to move in any case, for my parents had endured my enforced stay at home wonderfully well and had been most understanding. I was not bringing in much money yet I was keeping myself, although I owed them more than I could give them at the time. Moreover, my two elder brothers were wondering what I was up to and one of them was very critical. They had left home some years earlier and knew nothing of what I was doing. I had told no one about my coaching and my writing, and they probably thought I had been spending my time idling and dreaming. The writing was too personal, too secret, to tell anyone about it. I had put all my stakes on it. It was, in fact, a bid for my life, the reason for my existence even at this stage. After the tremendous energy that had gone into it during the past few months I was satisfied in my own mind that I had made the right choice. I kept it secret because I did not want to waste energy by meeting the inevitable doubts and objections; and my instinct to keep it close was the right one. At last I was single in my mind: 'Blessed is the man who has found his work, let him ask no other blessing.' Therefore I was more armoured than I had once been. I knew it would be a long haul to gain any success in writing, and I would certainly not make much money from it and would probably have to have a contributory job as well. Yet I believed I would eventually attain it. I recall, in the early days after leaving university when the way failed to open out, the future had looked very bleak indeed. I was looking over some of my books and I came across a book of criticism of the *Georgics* and in it I found an inspiriting quotation that served as a beacon to my fading belief in myself and in everything else. The writer maintained that Virgil's message was this: 'Find out what you have to do and do it with all your might. The powers that rule the world are fundamentally just and you will get your reward.' I would go up to London once more and put this philosophy to the test.

The ten o'clock train from Fishguard to London was full by the time it stopped at Cardiff where I boarded it. It appeared that other people were leaving south Wales as well. This was the peak period of the migration from the valleys as well as from west Wales: hundreds of thousands left during the years of the great diaspora. Most took one-way tickets, as I did. There was no coming back. I sat on my suitcase in the corridor and I soon had some company there, when we stopped at Newport. Fortunately, except for a brief halt at Reading there was no other stop until we got to Paddington. Although not every one of my journeys to this station had been successful, I always reacted positively when I arrived there. There was a hopeful air of bustle about the G.W.R. terminus that, it seemed to me, other metropolitan stations did not have. There was always plenty of light in the station: it was not dark and gloomy like Liverpool Street, which someone described as sited like an ominous dragon at the portal to discourage the invasion of East Anglia. Something, too, can be attributed to Paddington's lightness and cleanliness by the fact that the prevailing south-west wind blows all the soot and smoke away from this side of the city.

I had written again to Ken, one of my younger brothers, and he had fixed me up for a week with a friend of his landlord's in Shepherd's Bush. I had £2 or £3 after paying my fare and I estimated that I would have to find some sort of job within the week or else I should be in queer street. I arrived on a Sunday and I planned to start the hunt for a job on the next day. My landlady, Mrs Lambert, with whom I was to stay, and her husband were sterling people. Mr Lambert was an old soldier who had a weak chest as a result of being in a gas attack during the war. They had a son who had just left home and got married. He had vacated his room for a friend who worked with him as a milkman and got up at five o'clock every morning. He was quite happy to allow me to share his room for a week. He was a Welshman, Jim Price, from Pembroke Dock. The wartime naval establishment there had been either reduced or closed down, and it was just another town that had hundreds of unemployed. Jim Price was one of the west Wales people who had caught a London train a few months earlier. He told me his story on the first night I met him—just to cheer me up, as he said! He was a short, wiry man about my age with a gingery fairness often found in people from south Pembrokeshire. When he got to London he soon had no money at all, and slept out in Hyde Park, newspapers around his legs and body to keep warm. He managed to get something to eat from the Salvation Army; and for a time it was tougher than he could have imagined. But he had one contact, a man from west Wales who kept a retail milk shop; and after hanging on for a few weeks, through him he got taken on as a roundsman by the Wilts United Dairies. That was my one conversation with him of any length. For I crept into bed at my normal hour during the week of my stay. He was already asleep as he was a very early riser.

Mrs Lambert was a cheerful, fair-haired woman. I was invariably lucky with my London landladies; and Mrs Lambert was no exception. The only thing I regret was that I did not ask her in which Suffolk village she had been born. It would have been a real pleasure to visit her relations in later years when we lived as a family in Suffolk and got to know and like the Suffolk people very much. One remarkable thing about her village was that she received by post every week about a dozen double-yolked eggs. I did not know that it was possible to have eggs with double yolks in such quantity: I always thought that a double yolk was a rare freak but I saw their size and tasted the double yolks which she assured me came every week without fail.

I had one of them next morning for breakfast and set off early for the West End. The plan I had formed was a bold one, and quite unreal as it turned out. It was to go to a few newspaper offices in Fleet Street and to walk in fearlessly and ask for a job—any job. Fleet Street was more or less as I had first seen it ten years earlier except that the *Daily Express* building—Beaverbrook's glasshouse—had sprung up and now dominated the other buildings. I stood for a while watching the people arriving at the office and I decided I had better wait for them to settle down. The newspaper men looked a seedy lot, though some of the younger ones were fresh and bouncing. In the first office I entered I saw the weakness of my plan. I met a young man just inside at an office at the front of the building: he had obviously been placed there to deal with, among other things, unannounced callers such as myself. I asked him whether I could see the staffing manager: What did I want him for? What should I want him for! For a job! He shook his head: 'There's no chance. I may as well tell you now.' He was the Cerberus. His brief was to keep callers away and it was no use blaming him. The bold approach would not work. You'd got to have the ear of someone inside first. I left him and tried one or two more newspapers but entry was as closely guarded as prisons.

The only chance of getting a job was through the *Sunday Referee*, the firm who had paid me a few cheques. But I had an irrational reluctance to approach the *Referee* because my relationship with them was tenuous and it might cease altogether if I turned up on their doorstep with my request. Moreover, I did not even know the name of the member of their staff who dealt with that section of the paper and I should hardly be likely to get farther than the front desk.

After a morning's marching around, I decided to take a break for a snack. In the afternoon I went into a labour exchange and a clerk gave me the tip that they were taking on men at the Post Office at Mount Pleasant. I walked there and found that the vacancies, mostly unskilled jobs, had been filled. Next I heard there were vacancies down in Whitehall in the Ministry of Agriculture and Fisheries. I walked down through Trafalgar Square, found the building and went through what seemed miles of corridors to an office where I met a big genial man who was helpful but regretted that all the temporary clerks' jobs had been filled. My first day's search had not been successful, but I had learned one fact. There was no profit in searching blindly for jobs and it was a pipe-dream to think that I could get something even vaguely connected with writing. Thinking it over that night I made no headway, and finally exhausted by the day's tramping, I must have fallen asleep soon after my room-mate. In the morning, fortified again by another of Mrs Lambert's double yolks I set off again. My plan had changed. If I compromised with my original idea not to take a teaching job, it might solve the difficulty: I decided to look for a job teaching physical education. I would then be able to fit my writing into the evenings and the week-ends. I would keep myself fit and would escape the awful tedium of being shut in a classroom with thirty or forty children, as I would spend a great deal of the time outdoors. It was a possible solution and I acted upon it immediately. Evening classes were now starting for the winter, and there was a chance that one of the organizations that ran classes in physical training might need someone. I was not far from Tottenham Court Road and I had the inspiration of calling at the Y.M.C.A. nearby. It must have been a true inspiration for it was one of the most decisive calls I have ever made.

The result was not 'no' but a kind of extended development of 'yes' through a remarkable man, Herbert Naylor, who was the Y.M.C.A. secretary at the time. I told him what I was seeking, and he was immediately responsive. There was no job going at the time as all the positions had been filled for the coming session. But he was far from dismissive and told me: 'I'm just going across to lunch. Would you care to come with me? We can then talk over the position.' He took me across to the Corner House where Tottenham Court Road joins Oxford Street. We entered and went through a shop straight into a huge luncheon room. While we were eating he told me about his son who was about my age. He was obviously concerned about him: 'Like you he's been having a difficult time.' His son was being harassed by his senior at work, and he was making life at work a burden. He had gained some comfort by reading the _Meditations_ of Marcus Aurelius, the Stoic emperor. (By coincidence, the next day I saw a sixpenny copy of the book outside a shop in the Charing Cross Road and bought it.) After lunch we crossed the street and returned to Mr Naylor's office. He told me that although he could not offer me a job there was one way out. There was a refresher course for youth leaders and teachers of physical education that had just started in a place not far from London Bridge. He was almost certain he could get me on the course if I should care to consider it. The course was not a long one but it was intensive. He suggested that I should return the following day and he could tell me the details. I agreed to do this.

My meeting with Herbert Naylor started a new hope that I would escape the end-of-the-week dilemma when all my money had run out. There were three days to go: I had arranged to stay with the Lamberts until Sunday at the latest, and I was determined that I would not impose on them with what was only a temporary arrangement. During the past few months I had cut my physical needs to a minimum and I could live very cheaply. I had lived near the bone but it was impossible for me to stay in London without a place to sleep. I could not live rough as Jim Price did: I was not tough enough.

I saw Herbert Naylor the next morning and he told me that I could go on the refresher course that had just started for teachers of physical training. It would mean, however, staying till the course finished at the beginning of March. If I accepted the offer he was sure that I would have no difficulty in getting a post as soon as the course finished. I could see immediately the argument for accepting the offer: in the interval that had elapsed since I left college and went on a previous course, I was badly in need of a refresher. Yet I had no money to pay for such a course. He said there would be no difficulty about that. There was a new drive for physical education which I had read about and I was struck by a phrase an educationalist had used in connection with it. He had maintained that the youth of the country suffered from 'physical illiteracy'. Herbert Naylor had been in touch with an organization that was enthusiastic about promoting this new drive and they would grant me a bursary. After discussing the proposal with him briefly, he suggested that I should go off for a couple of hours. He did not want me to make up my mind immediately but I should have time to think it over.

I left him just after noon and made my way to the British Museum. I took him literally, and had two hours to do it in. The alternatives firmly in my mind, I drifted towards the Roman rooms of the Museum which were then on the ground floor not far from the entrance. At least I could come to a decision in more or less familiar surroundings. On a question of such moment, I found it almost impossible to think around every argument logically, step by step, holding the various considerations rationally in the forefront of my mind and going through the arguments with objective precision. I could hold the argument for brief periods and then the mind would slide away, diverted by one of the exhibits before me. Then my purpose would suddenly become uppermost again and I would be called back to the need to clamp down on the alternatives. If I accepted Herbert Naylor's proposal, it would mean my giving up the idea of writing, at least temporarily. I would have to keep my tender plant at a lower temperature for the duration of the course and probably for some time afterwards. Yet my natural impatience after I had made a start—a creditable start at writing, although no real success had come—made me fret at the tyranny of circumstances. It was like walking round the foot of the mountain before I was allowed to climb the lower foothills. But what was the alternative? To be on my uppers with no money and no hard plans—down and out, and if not completely out, perilously near it.

I noticed the Roman alphabet printed out in cursive script in a glass case. For the best part of half an hour my thoughts slipped away again from the gnawing at my problem: I had not seen the cursive script put down so clearly. That might be useful at some time, and I took out a notebook and began to make a copy. I have the original still, frozen as the record of another sort, and festooned with invisible thoughts about my dilemma and later thoughts about my immaturity. But was it a real dilemma? It was more like old Hobson's choice again, the usual one-way alternative that seemed to figure in my life. It was only the illusion of a decision. But at least I had been through the motions. Hobson, though, could be looked at in another way. Perhaps after all he was the convenient curtailer of embarrassing choices, impelled by my own good daimon to be in the long run a real benefactor. I had finished copying the script and I closed my notebook. It was time to make my way back and tell Herbert Naylor that I had made up my mind to go on the course.

Having made the decision, I was easier in my mind. I was more sure I could get a job. What sort of job was not of first importance as long as I was able to press on with the writing. I would have to learn patience and to think in terms of years and not weeks and months. I ended my week with the Lamberts with mixed feelings, and travelled down to Southwark on the Sunday. The hostel where the course members were staying was in Trinity Square in the Borough. It was an early nineteenth-century square with well built Georgian terraced houses, and we were in one that was big enough to hold most of the twenty-nine men who were on the course. A large proportion of them were ex-regular soldiers, men who had served seven years abroad and were now in the reserve. A number of them had been in the Indian army, and some of them had served in the Far East. They had all done physical training as part of their military service and a few of them had specialized in it; all were now being trained as leaders of boys' clubs and groups of unemployed that were being formed all over the country. There were also two or three atypical members like myself who joined the course after it had started. One was an athlete about my age. He had been a stockbroker and given up his career to start a new one. Another mysterious member turned up to take part in the morning sessions. He was a man of about twenty-eight who was dressed in an impeccable City uniform: dark suit, white shirt, and bowler hat. He was just about to be married (though I feel sure that a physical training course had not been prescribed particularly for that). He was said to have a private income and that his father was Master at one of the Cambridge colleges. He was a good mixer. One of his favourite tricks after a morning's vigorous programme was to take his leave by somehow bouncing his bowler hat on his arm in a gesture often performed by music-hall comedians—and afterwards guiding it on to his head, raising it ceremoniously again to wish us a humorously formal goodbye. The gymnasium where we spent most of the day was in Tooley Street near London Bridge, a very busy street where heavy dock-loads drawn by brisk teams of horses were continually passing. The gymnasium was a quarter of an hour's brisk walk from the hostel, passing through the rather grim streets of Bermondsey.

While I was on the course I occasionally went up to the West End but I found it more absorbing to explore Southwark itself, with its cathedral and Chaucerian links; and to cross London Bridge and explore the deserted City. In the early Thirties, before the bombings of the second war, the City was full of Johnson and Dickens associations. Yet it was the alive, overall penumbra of the surrounding old buildings rather than any specific landmark that impressed me most of all. For the City on a Sunday was a haunt of ghosts. On this day it was deserted by its people. The actual inhabitants were only a few hundreds, and those seemed to be resting, giving place to all those 'echoes' that were the City's real inhabitants to wander silently, unseen and unmolested, pausing in the courts and alleys and entering the churches. The narrow streets around St Paul's were thick with associations that made the City and the Borough—in spite of their gloom and periodic fogs—infinitely more rewarding even to live in than the soulless suburbs. The grimy offices and squares, the churches and historic buildings were instinct with their long and rich shoulder-rubbing with history.

Yet I felt that living in London was like living in the centre of a kind of reality: you could not stand too much of it. It was not a place for poor people. Ideally, it was only for those who were rich enough to ration themselves with prescribed doses and who could retreat into the country and become revitalized by long withdrawals. Yet the real Londoners, the people we were meeting at that time in the Borough, Bermondsey, the Old Kent Road, the Elephant and Castle, and the City, subsisted, inured through long genetic adaptation to the environment that could wear out incomers in a bare generation. They were the drawers on a gene bank that had lasted—was it conceivable?—since before the Romans discovered the settlement they had christened Londinium. David Jones the poet, whose father came from north Wales and whose mother was the daughter of a Deptford shipmaster, would have had no difficulty in accepting such a thesis.

One of the great rallying aphorisms of this time was an ancient one: *mens sana in corpore sano* (a sound mind in a healthy body). Yet this was not as straightforward as it appeared in the form in which it was usually quoted. As Juvenal wrote it, its context was much wider: *orandum est ut sit mens sana corpore sano.* This is something very different from the partial quotation: good health is not something that is given. It does not follow automatically that you have a sound mind if your body is sound. If you strive for total health, the striving alone will not ensure that you gain it. It is open to the influence of other factors, other contingencies; and to attain it it has to be prayed for—*orandum est*: which is only another way of saying that you may have to strive for health, for mental or spiritual equilibrium—in spite of all the difficulties and disabilities—and rest in hope and in faith that it will be given to you.

The phrase came up in my mind and became linked with my own dilemma: if I was to be involved in a cynical preparation for the coming war how was I to reconcile it with the Greek ideal of physical fitness, fitness for its own sake? My only available technique for dealing with this dilemma, had I known it, was to place it in a wider setting, to remove it from the supposed purity of moral isolates like 'good' and 'pure' and to place it in a pragmatic context where daily living forces us to deal with logically irreconcilable opposites as best we can.

My friend Bill Evans inadvertently gave me an object lesson in this. We met in London when the Welsh team came to Twickenham. After the match, we went to a pub near Piccadilly and I told him I was convinced that Hitler would start another war. He disbelieved me; and I told him that the course I was on convinced me that preparation for another war had already started in Britain. He asked me then: 'Do you really believe there'll be another war?' On my telling him I did, he answered in words that were typical of him: 'If that's so, it's me for the long grass!' He would not let anything that would happen in a few years' time disturb his good-humoured acceptance of day-to-day. In the event, when the war did come he spent it in the Far East with the R.A.F. in an area that was not particularly outstanding for its cover of 'long grass'; and he did not return here until the war was over. I was much happier after my talk with Bill. His attitude was much more fitting for my problem than the casuistical wrestling with absolutes that I had been indulging in. His humorous phrase about taking cover was a better tactic than trying to line up all one's future problems, ticking them off in quite theoretical order.

The following month I visited Bill and his mother in Cambridge. My first impression of the scene was not of the buildings or even the immemorial elms but of the people. There were a number about, visitors like myself going round the colleges in the sunshine, young undergraduates showing their parents around, some walking with their girls, some in groups walking through a college court as though to visit a friend for a morning drink. We walked through King's College and across the river to the Backs where we saw the aconites just beginning to show themselves under the trees and being dutifully commented on as the first harbingers of spring. Later we went into King's Parade where morning service had finished at St Mary's and the people were coming out into the sunshine. As well as the casually dressed undergraduates walking about, there were two exquisitely attired young men threading self-consciously along the crowded pavement in the direction of Trinity Street. 'Probably going to the Pitt Club, a smart undergraduate club further up the street,' Bill told me after they had passed. Most of the crowd had been to morning service and were dressed conventionally in dark suits and the women in sober attire. The young men were on the whole above average height, healthy looking and well fed. Most of them wore casual jackets and grey flannels of good material, though their jackets showed leather patches at the elbows. Bill had been in Cambridge long enough to become familiar with some of the mores and he told me a few of them. Since the Second World War these fashions have changed considerably so I suspect that most of these quirks had long ago disappeared before the war was over; but I later confirmed two he mentioned on my first visit. A Cambridge man on meeting you for the first time—though undoubtedly this trait was not confined to Cambridge—would look at your tie, and when occasion offered would take a surreptitious glance at your shoes: for he considered the tie and the shoes an infallible method of social placing. Shabby clothes were not a sure guide. In a self-conscious society, as Cambridge was then, shoes and ties were certain first indicators of where you stood—on the right side of the class-line or well below it. But an attribute that was evident from my first visit—even before I met some of the university people—was their easy poise that bordered on arrogance.

In the Thirties a vast distinguishable majority had been to public schools and their manner was natural, inbred and not assumed. They had been conditioned by their upbringing to believe that they were predestined to become leaders of men: they had in effect a duty to take upon themselves the mantle of directors of society. They were to be the rulers. At the beginning of the century, and up to the First World War, the old order was a little dented but more or less intact. The public schools had continued in their élitist philosophy almost unquestioned. This was the basis of the classical training that was the core of the public school curriculum, along with a harsh, spartan discipline that induced in the majority of boys, who did not rebel against it, a tough insensitivity. It was the enshrinement of the Platonic philosophy that there are the leaders and those who are led; and that the leaders should be carefully trained after their choosing from a narrowly defined class. This was the keystone of the public-school system. The teaching of Latin and Greek, although excellent training for the understanding of language, had as its main purpose the instillation of the truth that the boys had been chosen as the leaders: this was the justification and the implicit message of the whole of their training. They had been picked out as 'guardians': although stripped of the Platonic disguise, their role was unashamedly that of the élite, extraordinary men whose purpose was to become pilots of society. The insensible conditioning throughout their life, and their partial insulation from the demands of daily living, had already thrust a role upon them.

To say that I consciously absorbed all this in my first visit would be wrong: much of my conviction was acquired within the next few years. Yet I was intuitively aware from the beginning that the whole scene was brittle and rooted in inequality; and my later experience made it difficult to find good reason for questioning my first impressions. It is true that many poor boys were picked out to become intercostal sinews in the British Empire but they were usually chosen at an impressionable age when the concept of empire was accepted uncritically. Many of them, being naturally attracted to the relaxed and gracious manner of living, became immovably fixed in the embrace of the world-view it represented.

I have often wondered about the reason for my adopting this rigidly nonconforming stance that was to be enhanced by many facets of life that I met when I first came to England. By nature I believe I have an easy-going streak: I have always been a better runner than a fighter. Yet one of the reasons for making me first bestir myself was that, even in the primary school, I realized that Wales had been given Cain's portion. Right through its history Wales has had to fight for its existence as a nation; at first through direct physical assault, later through having to resist the subtler appeal to its people to give up their nationhood and become 'English-like-us'. But Wales was the first of England's colonies and a Welshman cannot forget it. Welshmen were treated as a subject people whose nationhood was not fully recognized; or if it was, as latterly, it was out of policy and not out of real conviction. I am reminded of a nonconformist minister I heard speaking at a political rally in Pontypridd in 1936 or 1937 when the Empire, if not in its heyday, still had its flag flying very high. As he quoted the often heard boast that the sun never set on the Empire his comment was, 'I'm not surprised; God wouldn't trust it in the dark.' Not an unjust comment, for it is debatable whether the good done by the imperialist opening up of the world is not outdone by its shortcomings: whether the mainspring, the spread of trade, has not been weakened by the exploitation and consequent antagonism of the native peoples. Yet the Commonwealth aspect seems to have lasted precariously beyond the demise of the Empire itself, and is making a residual contribution to the eventual world government that is bound to materialize if there is to be a future at all for the human race.

After my first introduction to the medieval splendour, even nobility, of the Cambridge colleges, we went to Huntingdon Road where Bill's mother had established a modest Welsh enclave—precariously as it turned out. She had moved late in life; and a few years of suburban Cambridge, in spite of a few friends in the Welsh Society, determined her return to Pontypridd. She had been brought up in a different social scene and at her age she could not transplant to a culture so very different from her own. The plant had become more tender with age and could not adjust to the new soil; and eventually it became a matter of life and death that it should be returned to its natural habitat. She became very ill; and Bill was forced to take his mother back to Wales where she regained her natural rhythm and lived to an advanced age.

The week following my visit, Bill sent me a letter telling me that he had just been talking to the physical training organizer for Cambridgeshire. There was a vacancy in a new, experimental community centre and school. It was called a Village College and had recently been opened at Sawston by the Prince of Wales. Many of the staff were graduates and it would be worth my putting my name forward as I had a good chance of getting the post. My course was coming to the end, and the physical training organizer for Cambridge was present at the display that was its climax. I met him during the evening. His name was Henry Payne: he was a pleasant Yorkshireman and he virtually guaranteed me a job if I applied. I left London in better heart than I had been in when I came up a few months before.

When I arrived home I found that Syd, who had finished his teacher's training in the summer, was still out of work after getting a good honours degree in chemistry. Rachel—Ray—had followed our older sister Esme into nursing. Peter my youngest brother was still at the county school and Molly, the youngest of the family, was at a school near home. I told my parents that I had the offer of a post and should start within the next few weeks. I wrote immediately to Henry Payne to tell him that I should be applying for a post in Cambridgeshire; and within a few days I received a form of application. I sent it in; and having the idea for a short story I settled down one morning with a blank sheet of paper, the writer's nightmare, before me. I had battered out a couple of sentences when I was interrupted by a knock at the door. It was a girl from the post office with a telegram. I was to attend an interview at the Shire Hall, Cambridge on the following Monday.

cambridge

# 8 · I Find What I Want

Although this interview happened so long ago, it is as cleanly etched on my mind and as fresh as if it were a picture I had seen last week. The Education Office was in the Shire Hall, a new, clean-lined, functional building at the top of Castle Hill within a hundred yards of the motte of the old Norman castle. The room of the interview was draped with thick, expensive curtains, and there were two oil paintings at each side of a large window—paintings with dark, long-legged matchstick figures in an industrial scene. But the room and its furniture were only a momentary, half-conscious impression that was filled in later. It was the man behind the desk, Henry Morris, the Education Secretary, who held my attention. He was tall with straight, dark hair and strikingly blue eyes, emphasized by a shirt of the same colour. His greeting, his relaxed manner, his well cut suit did not fit into the picture of the educational nabobs I had already met; and the informal, almost casual, tone of the encounter put me at my ease immediately. Henry Morris had my qualifications on the desk before him and he questioned me about some points, as though they had just come up in a pleasant conversation. He occasionally turned to Henry Payne for elucidation. There seemed little connection between the pleasantness of the talk and the importance it had to me at this point in my career. It was as though this conversation had already been rehearsed and this was a performance where there would be no fluffs and would run to its proper end with uninterrupted smoothness. At one point, Henry Morris asked: 'You read classics at Cardiff: does that mean you can take up Virgil—for instance—put your feet up and enjoy him like an English book?' Having read a great deal of Virgil since leaving university, I truthfully said that I could. That seemed to impress him although it had no direct bearing on the interview as my application was simply for physical education and games. Yet the question was of a piece with the informality of the interview and I was prepared for the odd question thrown at me at a tangent. He turned to Henry Payne: 'We can send Mr Evans to Sawston, don't you think, Mr Payne?' Then to me: 'When can you start?' I answered that I was ready to start immediately; and he picked up the telephone and asked his deputy to spare him a moment.

I learned later that Mr Hodge, a plain affable man with a round head, was Henry Morris's Sancho Panza. He was a Lancastrian, as Morris was himself, and his main job was to be his second and break-fall on his ambitious forays on the educational front, especially at the beginning of his campaign when he met with so much opposition. The paintings I had noticed in the office were also by a Lancastrian, L. S. Lowry, whose patron Morris had become long before he was famous. He had bought so many of Lowry's paintings in the Twenties and Thirties that they became an embarrassment to the Education Committee when they soared in value after Henry Morris had died. They were in a dilemma whether to realize their market value or to accept the responsibility of letting pictures of such artistic interest remain in the Shire Hall and undertaking the security precautions that would entail. This pattern repeated itself in other aspects of Morris's life: his seeing long before others the beginnings of a talent or the need for a new departure, and having the courage and persistence to advocate its development in face of others' misgivings and even outright opposition. As long ago as the early Twenties he had appreciated what was happening in the English countryside. The old medieval framework of society had been breaking up for a long while, but the war that had just finished had quickened the process. Mainly owing to the stress of the war itself, technology developed a determined spurt so that when it was over certain side effects of the new technology became apparent.

The most epoch-making was the development of the internal combustion engine with its ability to annihilate distance. To Morris, appointed Education Officer in the Twenties to a rural county, it must have occurred with the force of a revelation that the new possibilities of motor transport had effectively broken down the isolation of the country village. As had happened in south Wales, when the war was over entrepreneurs, like small village business men or soldiers discharged with a gratuity, began buying up surplus army vehicles that had been used on the Western Front; and they opened up rural routes, especially to the towns. Morris saw the social effect of this and its possibilities for education. The country village, while apparently going on its leisurely pace that had remained in essence unchanged since the Middle Ages, had suffered in the revolution. The new form of transport now placed the village on the town's doorstep. This changed status of the rural village was already showing up the inadequacy of its old institutions, especially the village schools. Morris was struck by the low standard of the rural schools that had been worsened by the recent war, and their remoteness and lack of the facilities compared with the more favoured town schools where education was beginning to be geared to the new technology. His solution was to concentrate education of the older pupils in the countryside; to select a site in a suitable large village, and to group a number of villages, usually ten, around it.

On this site, therefore, a community centre was to be built to serve the group of villages and to act as a focus to dissuade people from drifting to the towns. Part of this social centre—the main part—was to be the school for the older pupils. The new buses made possible the attendance not only of the pupils during the day, but the adults during the evening. In this way Morris hoped to resuscitate some of the life that had already drained from the rural village into the towns.

This pattern of rural education envisaged by Morris in the mid-twenties is a commonplace today, but it was viewed then by many as a shattering threat to the social order of the countryside, an order that had served adequately for so long. Morris was looked upon either as a red-hot revolutionary, or pin-pointed as another Don Quixote tilting vainly at cardboard windmills. The fact was that he had made a true reading of rural history, and he believed passionately in the way he thought village education should go. He was determined, and he would not be diverted from his course: it was to be his life's mission. With the help and support of understanding people connected with the University of Cambridge he got the Cambridgeshire Education Committee to approve the plans of the first of the new centres. It was to be called a village college and was to be built at Sawston, a few miles south of Cambridge, a largish village containing a well-known papermill and a glove industry. The building was in a rural setting and Henry

Morris, in his 'William Morris' guise, insisted that it should be of good design, well furnished, with good interior decoration, consonant with his ideal that children deserve a good physical environment. He saw that they absorbed part of their education unconsciously from their early environment, and good design was therefore an integral part of a child's emotional growth. In this, which made him unique among pioneers in education, Morris had the support of well-known artists, architects and writers like Herbert Read, Maxwell Fry and Walter Gropius who designed the last of the pre-war village colleges in the late Thirties before he went to America after the break-up of the German Bauhaus. As far as education was concerned, Morris's emphasis on good design was responsible for an international change in attitude towards educational buildings, so that they were no longer regarded simply as 'institutions' but as an opportunity to make a vital contribution to the humane development of all the people who used them.

But all this was, as far as I was concerned, in the future. I was impressed with Morris's generosity as a man in that he allowed me to begin earning immediately although it was only a few weeks from the end of the term. Of the background of his beliefs and the enthusiasm that generated them I was entirely ignorant, yet I warmed to him as someone who wasn't 'stuffy', who was an artist and went to the essentials and side-stepped the conventions of how, for instance, an interview should be managed. Coming away from Shire Hall I had a good feeling; and Bill and his mother were delighted at my news. I stayed another night with them, and the next morning Henry Payne took me to the village college at Sawston. I met the warden and managed to get lodgings a few hundred yards away.

At last I had got myself a job. Recently I discussed this period of my life with a friend who told me something that made me look back with a new enlightenment. After he left university in the Thirties he had been employed in education. He told me: 'The difficulty facing Welsh teachers in getting jobs in England was even worse than you may have thought. When I was on the education side of local government in the city of—(in the south of England) from 1937 to 1940, my boss instructed me to throw out all applications from Welsh teachers when we were considering replies to our advertisements, even those writing in England who had given their houses Welsh names! We always considered that Wales had over-produced teachers. You were lucky to find yourself in touch with someone as enlightened as Henry Morris.'

I had thus reached a new stage in my life with hope and a little apprehension. The reservation came later when I reminded myself that my good fortune in getting a post would contribute only indirectly to my main endeavour: I still had to get on with my chosen job of writing. Yet I met this with impatience and brushed it aside. I had solved one problem at least, and would have to be satisfied with that and bide my time as best I could. Here again, I had come up against something that I have called my daimon, some deep-down principle of movement that I had often been resentful of, and even opposed, but that I eventually came to recognize, in the light of a fuller understanding, as being entirely on my side. It was the true arbiter of the way I should go, even if I met resistance from my everyday self that had a conscious impulse to stick its heels in and to follow the 'sensible' way. I was again backing my other self: only time would tell whether or not I had made the right choice.

I went home for the Easter holidays and felt more relaxed: I could now escape the questioning of insensitive and curious acquaintances. I now had a responsible job. A few days after I arrived home, I met Jim Adlam through my neighbour Harry Jeffreys. He, too, had come from his native Somerset into the valleys when he was a young man. He had the reputation among his mates of being 'long-headed': he was a great reader of books. Like many of the older miners, he had a disease of the lungs and had finished working. He was thin-faced and had a good forehead. He was invariably dressed in an old, much faded overcoat. His later reading was almost solely philosophy and the economics of the miners' struggle. He had a biting, satirical wit and was known as a freethinker, a label that was much used at the beginning of the century. He once told me that a clear-sighted view of religion was the beginning of social criticism. He would ask: 'What is the term 'agnostic' they are fond of using? An agnostic is nothing but an atheist in a top hat.' In discussion, his emaciated face would light up. He was like a medieval anchorite who followed the philosophy that little eating makes for much thinking. He told me that his father had been gardener to Edward Augustus Freeman, the Victorian historian. Freeman had been at Trinity College, Oxford, though he had a house near Bath; and it is probable that contact with the historian gave the young Adlam respect for learning.

A short while afterwards, I was walking on the hills and came across him again. He was squatting on the lee side of a drystone sheep wall with three of his neighbours, all miners. They were arguing about Tommy Farr's—the Rhondda boxer's—chances against the American, Joe 'Lueese'. The one who talked most knowledgeably about the boxer was a thickset man, Joe Lloyd, with the telltale blue miner's scar on his hands and face. He was a haulier underground and of the classical stamp for that job, strongly built and short, so that he could put his shoulder under a tram of coal and lift it on to the rail once it had gone off. I had already met Dai Williams who worked on the night shift at the colliery. He was sitting next to a quiet man Jim Adlam addressed as Gilbert. Jim Adlam told me about Gilbert later. He was an out-of-work miner and like Jim, a great reader. He was an admirer of the eighteenth-century Irishman Bishop Berkeley, who believed that the only things that have 'reality' are the ideas that are present in the mind. He denied the existence of matter, which he dismissed by ingenious arguments. Gilbert's uncle was a Church in Wales clergyman in a nearby valley and occasionally he helped his nephew with the gift of a pound or two. Gilbert would celebrate this with a few glasses of beer. He then got very argumentative and would make a thrust at Adlam, telling him that his materialism, in spite of its name, had no real substance. Now idealism was fire on Jim Adlam's skin and he countered Gilbert's argument with the unfeeling contempt that Dr Johnson used when he refuted the Bishop by kicking a stone into the gutter. But the arguments they had under the sheep-wall were just interludes to help them through the empty days. Real quarrelling was a needless waste of heat; and Gilbert always returned to his place under the wall even after the fiercest argument that ended with Jim's Parthian shot: 'Now tell me, Gilbert, how *real* do you think your uncle's bonus is?'

My first term at Sawston passed very agreeably. I coached a few of the older boys as sprinters and they managed to win a cup in an inter-school competition. The following term, the community centre's activities started. These adult classes were the characteristic mark of the new experiment and great importance was given to them by Henry Morris because they were, in essence, the justification of the village college concept. His belief was that by the twentieth century the rural village, still medieval in its basic pattern, had lost its focus, especially in its social aspect and that it needed a substitute organization for the Church that the village colleges could supply.

My job was to run classes of young men in physical education with a recreative bias. I enjoyed doing this and later at the suggestion of the organizer I combined classes from three different villages as an experiment. All went well, apparently, during the first hour of the class but after the break-interval only about half the class reappeared. On going to find out the reason I questioned one of the defecting group:

'We are not going to spend the rest of the evening with *foreigners*.' This was my first lesson in inter-village rivalry that was so intense fifty years ago. The missing half of the class came from the really rural villages that extended to the Essex border. The others came from the villages that bordered on the borough of Cambridge; Grantchester, Shelford and Stapleford. Although some of these villages were barely three or four miles apart, the old feeling that the people in the next village were strangers still existed. This was proof of Henry Morris's theory that already, at that time, the end of the First World War, the internal combustion engine had rendered the largely self-supporting village community an anachronism. It was at least another generation later before Morris's ideas became generally accepted. In those areas where village colleges have been going for half a century, this intense parochialism died a natural death.

The staff at Sawston was an atypical one. The teachers who had come straight from college or university were in the minority. Three had served in the 1914–18 war and two others had been in industry. Therefore the staff as a whole had a fairly wide experience of out-of-school life and this was very salutary, and the occasional staff-room discussions often transcended the usual shoptalk that was the bane of a close community. There were two or three graduates; one was a Londoner who had spent a year in Kingsley Hall, an East End settlement, before coming to Sawston, She later became my wife. She was brought up as a Quaker and in spite of the difference of some of our views we found that we had a strong area of agreement. The teaching conditions, as could be expected in a new building, were excellent except that there were, finally, more pupils than it was originally designed for. Yet in the economic climate of the time restrictions had to be accepted if not with good grace at least with an understanding of their cause. One important item of equipment, however, was included: a metalwork shop where an early tractor was installed so that country boys should have a basic knowledge of a fairly new, though by no means common, piece of farming equipment. There were complaints from some of the local farmers in the county that these boys' fathers had followed the horse-plough all their lives and it was likely that their sons would continue to do the same. In the light of the depressed state of East Anglian farming at the time, such a complaint was understandable. A few years later, however, when the outbreak of war brought new life to farming, many of the boys were using tractors in their work and were very grateful for their early introduction to its mechanism. This was another small instance of Morris's knack of seeing farther than the economic malaise that had affected farming at the time the village college scheme started.

near Abercynon

Sawston

# 9 · *A Family of Our Own*

At first I was completely taken in by Cambridge: I was like a visitor
seeing the glamorous part of the town only, and revelling in the colleges
and the wonder of a long historical tradition that was studded by the
names of great men over the centuries—a wonder that still persists in
spite of my now seeing Cambridge plain. I envied the students who
strolled so nonchalantly through the streets or hurried off to their
lectures. They had a studied air as though they were conscious of their
apartness. If you came into contact with the better sort of them, the often
casual negligence of their dress and their remote friendliness appeared
almost as though they were consciously trying to mask the exclusiveness,
the class arrogance of the more exhibitionist, the more indecent of their
fellows. Yet all acted out of a feeling of having a secure position in
society, whether inbred or newly acquired and therefore rather brittle;
and this demonstrated what a cancer was at the root of our
class-infected society that places like Cambridge unconsciously
prolong.

On my first acquaintance with the scene I was content to accept it at
its face value, exploring its buildings, its museums and bookshops,
absorbing the novelty of living in a unique community that I could
observe from the outside. Bill Evans had joined the university to read for
another degree but I had no ambition to do this. All my efforts, apart
from the necessity of earning, went into writing: I was quite immune to
the idea of academic advancement.

The experiences I had later confirmed my initial feeling about the whole Cambridge scene. On returning to Sawston after one of my vacations, I wrote to the Trinity man whose name I had from William Gallacher, the Communist M.P. whom I had met at a Cardiff conference during the holidays. Presently I received an answer from a woman who turned out to be his sister. She was the wife of the Communist organizer of the area. She suggested that I should meet her in Lyons café in Petty Cury which was at that time a popular meeting place for Peace Pledge members and trade unionists. She asked me where I was working, and then advised me to contact the secretary of a group that met in the house of a railway driver in Cherry Hinton. I cycled over after school to meet the group. Albert Brown was a train-driver on the Cambridge–Liverpool Street line. Owing to shiftwork he could only rarely attend the meetings in his house. The Browns had a lodger, a science research student, a short man with clean-cut, positive opinions who gave the impression of having everything weighed up and settled. There was also another scientist who was a member of the group. He was very articulate but was kept in his place by his wife who was even more articulate. She had in addition a very prim manner of speech acquired, I suspect, through speaking to women's groups in the university. There was another woman, a dentist. We spent the time discussing the sale of 'literature' and listening to short talks that each member of the group prepared in turn. I attended this group for a couple of months, and although I did not admit it to myself at the time, I felt that the university members were getting a new thrill through posing as crypto-Communists or revolutionaries. Three of them had assumed names and insisted on being called by them during the meeting. This experience, although it may have been necessary in Cambridge, did not square with my experience of Communists in south Wales, where there had been an unashamed openness. I recognized that they had to be cautious, but I had the feeling that they were partly taken in by the conspiratorial attraction of owning a pseudonym. Fortunately, I was directed to a group that met in the county of Cambridgeshire. It was composed chiefly of middle-class professional people from the eastern counties. It was a more high-powered cell that met at a village called Horningsea in a period house that was near the river. It was owned by the leader of the group: very fittingly it had monastic associations and there were some old inscriptions on the wall that seemed to prove it.

Work at the village college was at high pressure and it was complicated by overcrowding, and in my case by the absence of a gymnasium. We had to use the school hall that we shared with the girls. A great deal of my time was spent in boring class-room work. It became increasingly difficult to balance the claims of the job, the writing, and my conviction that I could not turn my back on the issues of the day. These became more pressing as the international situation worsened and the invasion of the Spanish Republic came as a foretaste of Hitler's and Mussolini's intentions in Europe. Under pressure of the work we were eager to escape from the village college after working double shifts on two days during the week. At first I went into Cambridge and met Bill Evans. But his mother became ill and he was increasingly involved in his domestic problem. Finally, having finished his degree, he got a post back in Pontypridd and took his mother home. By this time we were seeing little of one another. Our interests had greatly changed since we were at college together. I recognized that I was a different person while Bill remained essentially the same with the same interests and the same horizons.

In the meantime I became friendly with the Quaker Florence Knappett. I noticed that we were usually on the same side in staff-room discussions and that she was a discriminating reader. Later we used to cycle round the countryside of south Cambridgeshire, often going down into Essex. Or we went to the Cosmopolitan cinema in Cambridge to see the foreign films that were often shown there. We often discussed books. Florence was an admirer of Jane Austen and one day when we were in London we went to see a dramatization of *Persuasion*. Emlyn Williams was in the cast, but I was mildly bored. Her novels were innocent of the kind of social content that I demanded at that time; they were too remote and apolitical, side-stepping the real issues of her time. It was not until thirty years later that I had forgiven Jane Austen her cosy, 'pastoral' reading of English society, and could unashamedly admit to Florence that Jane Austen's novels were faultlessly constructed and gave a convincing picture of a certain class but they would never quicken my pulse rate.

The book I was enthusiastic about then was by the editor of *Labour Monthly* and I pressed Florence to read it. It nearly caused a rift, for it was like inviting her to a meal of chopped straw. For although Palme Dutt was a brilliant political analyst, his thoughts were wrapped up in a style so costive that it demanded intense application to fathom them. I sensed from her comments that Palme Dutt would be no rival to Jane Austen and I ceased to be his advocate. Yet at this period I was insensitive to other people's thoughts about the political situation and the coming war and would wade into any discussion without realizing that other people did not have the same urgency about what was happening. In fact I had become a sort of political hot-gospeller. Although stopping short of recommending to my friends and whoever would listen what they must do to be saved, in my naïvety and inexperience I thought that I had only to convince people with well marshalled reasons and compelling arguments about the likely course of events for them to agree with me forthwith. I was naïve in that reason alone is not sufficient to impel action or even a change of attitude. Only when reason is buttressed by feeling, however arrived at, can it overcome the comfortable inertia of daily routine, thought and preoccupations.

The job went moderately smoothly. Sawston was an unusual school. The plan of the building was square with one open side. In the centre was a lawn and a fountain and on one arm were the class-rooms, faced on the other side by the adult wing, the visible basis of the claim to be a college. This arm of the building included a spacious library used by the village as well as the school. It was well stocked with County Library books around a nucleus of a hundred or so volumes of the Everyman Library, the gift of the publishers. Also in this wing was a medical room and the Walnut Room, so called from its tasteful panelling of that wood. It was used for special exhibitions and lectures, and for meetings of the governing body. The art exhibitions that Morris arranged in this room were particularly valuable. He got various bodies to exhibit; and I recall a particular show in the mid-Thirties that was given by the Council for Encouragement of the Arts, a forerunner of the Arts Council. They staged travelling exhibitions of British paintings among other shows. I remember one occasion when two painters, I believe from the Essex village of Great Bardfield, lectured on some of the painting displayed; and I began to see that art was something more than a formal statement hanging on a wall. Lecturers from Cambridge often spoke in the Walnut Room and a popular one was Dr Shepherd, the Master of King's, who, sitting on a table, disguised his lecture as a comfortable chat. It was these little extra additions and the occasional communal event that made teaching at Sawston bearable. This breaking up of the school routine, by what some purists regarded as educational trimmings, placed the curriculum in a wider setting that made visual appreciation an essential ingredient of education.

In the early days of Sawston there was always an interesting stream of visitors for it was the first establishment of its kind. It was more than an experiment; as events proved, it was the shape of things to come. Visitors came from all over Britain and a fair number also came from abroad. Whenever he could get away from his office in Cambridge they were shepherded around by Morris himself, talking volubly and waving his arms about in expansive gestures in legitimate enthusiasm for his 'baby', the first of the village colleges he had in mind for the county. He would approach the gardening master at almost every visit, urging him to plant more flowers so that the whole building would be a 'blaze of colour'. This was typical of Henry Morris's concentration on the single objective, entirely disregarding things as they were. For the reality of the gardening master's job was to grow sufficient vegetables to provide a school dinner for most of the pupils and the staff. All this was incidental to his main job of teaching the boys gardening. He had an assistant who was on the job permanently, ensuring that the canteen had sufficient supplies of vegetables to provide a school dinner for the price of tuppence ha'penny. This was a very low price even for the early thirties. Rightly so, for the agricultural workers had—with the miners—the lowest wages of any workers. It was very noticeable in the children of workers from the southern villages that were really rural. The contrast with the children of the suburban villages of Shelford and Grantchester was most marked. I had noticed the undernourishment in some of the boys from the purely agricultural villages: they were often grossly underweight and their skin was pale and almost diaphanous. After I had been in the job for a couple of years the school had its first assessment. A posse of government inspectors descended on the school and stayed for a week. The man who inspected physical education was pleasant and more approachable than the average inspector. He told me he was surprised. 'I thought country boys would be more robust than this. Some of these boys look really weedy.' This was an accurate assessment. Many of them were just as undernourished as the boys from the south Wales valleys from which I had just come. It was a wry commentary on the state of farming at that period: on some of the richest and most productive arable farming areas of Britain many of the workers' children were virtually half-starved.

About this time it occurred to me on one of my vacations in south Wales that there would be themes for short stories in some of the tales I was hearing from Jim Adlam and his friends, and I purposely sought out their company and listened to their discussions on the hill above my home. They talked about football or boxing, and the farms round about, but especially about their work in the mines. Some of my early stories about the valleys came from Jim Adlam's company under the drystone wall. But the first story I had published, 'Red Coal', was used by Edgell Rickwood in *Left Review*. It was based on an incident told me by my brother-in-law Jack Bickham. For some reason that now escapes me I sent it in under a pseudonym. It stimulated one letter from an American publisher and another from a Welshman, Keidrych Rhys. Rhys was about to start the magazine *Wales* with a nucleus of writers that included Dylan Thomas, Vernon Watkins, Glyn Jones, Llewelyn Wyn Griffith and Idris Davies. The first number was all poems and he held my story over to the second. *Wales* was the beginning of a renaissance in writing in south Wales and I was proud to be a part of it. I got great satisfaction from these small achievements that stimulated me to carry on with my difficult balancing act of keeping my 'trinity' moving. I could not give any one of them up. Fortunately I was in good health and able to stand the pressure. Each time I came home to the valley from Cambridgeshire I had a new stimulus and a good break from which I returned refreshed.

More than once while making notes of my conversation with the miners it struck me that their accounts of the old methods of working the mines, just as mechanization was coming in, were valuable in that they gave authentic background material to any stories I would be moved to write. But more than this, the thoughts of the miners during this critical time, the rise of Fascism and the drift towards war, were extremely relevant to my own thoughts. It convinced me that the estimate of many of the thinking miners, their full appreciation of what was happening was far from negligible. Their thoughts were truer in fact—in view of what happened—than those of our rulers. But surely, it may be objected, it is nonsense to suggest that the opinions of ordinary people should be preferred to those of the statesmen, the experts. But the thinking miners of the thirties were not 'ordinary people'. They had been through lock-outs, strikes, depression and semi-starvation and they had become sensitized to the class structure of the country, particularly at a time when the prime minister himself was involved in iron and coal. This gave them a deep, often unexpressed knowledge of the divided consciousness of our rulers whose every action had to be balanced not by the sole consideration of the country's welfare but as much by their desire to preserve the advantages that had accrued to their own class.

Yet my pressing concern of the moment—to get background material for the writing of stories—did not allow the historical value of what they were giving me to come fully to the surface. The spirit of the time, and the preoccupation with the seeming inevitability of industrial strife and the coming war was clearly not favourable to recognizing potential historical data. All this stayed underground and did not show itself until it resurfaced nearly two decades later. By this time I was married and had a family and had gone to live in Suffolk; and there I talked with the farm workers and farmers exactly as I did with the miners in the valleys in the Thirties.

The Communist group's new meeting place was at Horningsea, a village a few miles down the river from the town. The leader, Joe Brereton, was Secretary of the Syndics of the Schools Examinations Board and there were also two other senior members of the University. One was Arthur Walton, an agricultural scientist who had been a conscientious objector during the First World War. Sometimes we met in his house on the research station. He had recently come back from a visit to Russia where he had made an estimate of the Soviet agricultural policy. The third Cambridge man was Hugh Sykes Davies, a lecturer in the English department of one of the colleges. He was a member of the Apostles, a secret society that had been in existence since Tennyson's time, and latterly included members of the so-called Bloomsbury group: Leonard Woolf, Desmond MacCarthy, Maynard Keynes, as well as the poet Rupert Brooke. The Apostles recently came into the news when it was known that Anthony Blunt was also a member. Our third don was also a surrealist poet and a humorist in a dry satirical vein. An appeal was once made to members for articles and short stories for a newspaper that was being distributed in the countryside. He capped the appeal with a few hints on the sort of material that was needed—for example, the Marxist way of sticking a cow! There were also members of the group who were at the tuberculosis settlement at Papworth. Two of these came from London and one from my home valley in south Wales. The discussions were more informed in this group; and our jobs were selling pamphlets in different parts of the county. Most of those involved were going out on week-ends to contact farm workers. Rarely did we meet one who was as politically conscious as the miners were. But most farm workers were well aware of their low wages and were ready to talk about the means of raising them. But on the whole they were suspicious of here-today-gone-tomorrow sellers of political literature—and rightly so—as I found out later when I got to know the East Anglian farm worker. I found that you have to be around for a very long time before you could influence him in any appreciable way.

I have often wondered since, what good the selling of political literature did, what proportion of it was read at all, and whether it contributed in any way to improving the farm worker's position. Were we just satisfying our own conscience in such an apparently unrewarding activity? Much of the seed got trodden underfoot but the odd grain undoubtedly took root and grew into a sturdy plant. I think that our small efforts in the Fens during the late Thirties were not in vain. Perhaps they helped to elect the local agricultural union's secretary into the 1945 Parliament.

near Ely

sawston

# 10 · The War

During the spring term Florence and I decided to get married. We had a long search to find somewhere to live. We thought we should like to live in Cambridge but getting a flat was almost impossible. Finally we found one at Trumpington, within easy cycling distance of school. On visiting it we found that it had not yet been converted into a flat but was simply the top half of a terraced house. Looking back, we should have been suspicious. Our 'landlord' who lived in the lower half of the house was a strange customer: he was a tough-looking Cockney who said he had been in the army in China and as proof of this showed me a huge scar on the forearm that had been caused so he said by a bayonet thrust. His wife was short and fat and had a little girl about two years of age, always clinging to her skirt. We were very doubtful of the set-up, but we were eager to get married and did not ask too many questions. The rent they asked was reasonable and we arranged with a plumber to install a kitchen sink and a gas stove in the rear room that we could use as a kitchen. Just before the end of term we bought some furniture, moved in and transferred our belongings, mainly books, from our lodgings and left for the holidays. I planned to go down to Abercynon while Florence went to her home in north London. We got married in a registry office, on a Saturday. Florence, now that she was married, had to give up her teaching job: this was a Board of Education ruling as there was so much unemployment among teachers.

We spent the week-end of the wedding putting up shelves and getting the flat into shape. On the Sunday evening we had two visitors: Keidrych Rhys, the editor of *Wales*, and a friend. They had motored up from London and were making for Cambridge. They had borrowed a car, and the engine had 'seized' and they were stranded. They had already been to my old digs and had been directed to the flat. Rhys's friend, a fair-haired young man called Barton, was obviously under the weather: they had been to a party the night before, and Barton was suffering from a hangover. There was nothing to do but improvise beds for them on the floor of the sitting-room.

We spent the evening listening to Rhys unfolding his plans for the magazine and talking about poetry and poets. We talked until midnight. Rhys was himself a poet and wrote a kind of surrealist verse of the kind that was fashionable in a small circle (most of the writers lived in London); but he was genuinely dedicated to poetry and he did a great service to encourage young writers in Wales at a particularly arid time for them. He was still talking poetry at breakfast. I had to cycle to work. Rhys and his friend were both broke and I was almost so myself, as it was the end of the month and my pay cheque was waiting for me at school. I had some loose silver in my pocket and they were able to catch a bus to Cambridge where they could rely on the freemasonry of the arts.

Florence and I did not stay in the flat long after that. We started looking for another place almost immediately. Our self-appointed 'landlord' was evidently a 'wide boy' as he would be known in his native East End. We made no enquiries about his status, but after we had been there for a couple of weeks we were able to assess the true position: he was an army pensioner who did not have a job. We had not been there a few days before he was touching me for a couple of pounds. Having seen the set-up below, of an incompetent housewife and a sickly child, we felt that we should not let caution temper our impulse to help. Shortly afterwards we had a visit from a middle-aged woman who lived three or four doors away. She was very upset, and went into a long explanation of the position. Our 'landlord' was simply her tenant and he had no authority to sublet the house. We did our best to pacify her, as she was very disturbed. She had just told her nephew, a big well built man, about the 'landlord' and he'd had a few words with him. The words led to fisticuffs and that is why events had come to a crisis. We told her we were moving out as soon as we could get another place. But we wondered why she had let the house to the Londoner in the first place. We decided that since the house was next door to a garage it was hard to let or sell, in spite of the rest of the property in the road being occupied by comfortable middle-class people. We managed very shortly afterwards to rent a bungalow half a mile away on the same road. The bungalow was called 'Kozy Kot' and had a yucca tree growing in the centre of the front lawn. At Sawston we heard a telling and amusing comment on the status of our road. The art mistress about this time moved to become principal of an art college in the Midlands. At the interview one of the women on the governing committee was a Cambridge graduate and asked her where she lived. On hearing that she lived on the Shelford Road in Trumpington, the committee woman raised her eyebrows: 'Not a very ... er ... amenable road for an art mistress.' I was just beginning to learn the surprising shades of the real Cambridge view of life.

By this time Sawston had lost its uniqueness. Two other village colleges had been built a few miles from Cambridge. We were spared some of Henry Morris's hypercritical attentions. Yet I got on moderately well with him as I divined in him a fellow-spirit, and was prepared to overlook his more palpable failings, the chief of which was an understandable impatience to get his sharp and socially valuable vision translated into practice. He had all the artist's striving for perfection, and anyone whose efforts fell below the ideal he had set himself would incur his displeasure. His taste in visual design was impeccable and when I later got to know something of him, I marvelled at his acquiring it and wearing it as someone who had been born with it, as unselfconsciously as his own skin. He never married and undoubtedly had homosexual tendencies, although they remained dormant and were never active, only betrayed, for example, by his contact with a woman driving a car. If she touched him inadvertently he overreacted and shied away from her as though he had been stung. I had a surprise when I later learned of Morris's background. I always assumed that he came from the 'top drawer', an expression that was often heard in the Cambridge of the Thirties. His accent, his demeanour, his clothes and his Trinity Street flat were, or seemed, absolutely in character. Yet he was a plumber's son from St Helen's in Lancashire, who started life as a reporter on a local newspaper. As a youth he decided to go in for the Church, and went to St David's College, Lampeter, in Wales to prepare himself. This was an Anglican foundation that was granted a charter early in the nineteenth century. His stormy-petrel temperament showed itself very early. He refused to comply with the Principal's fiat that the students, who at that time were almost solely theological, should oppose the Welsh Disestablishment Act, making the Church in Wales a separate body from the Anglican Church. Morris became unpopular and was assaulted by two or three students. He took them to court and won his case. But he was compelled to leave Lampeter, and went on to Oxford where he finished reading for a degree. War intervened and on coming out of the army he went into the administrative side of education.

Henry Morris was never easy in his personal relations. While we were at Sawston he appeared to have been socially ostracized by the Cambridgeshire establishment. He had socialist leanings and he had the reputation of being a difficult person to get on with, a natural outsider or individualist. The most telling analysis of Morris's type of character is contained in Edmund Wilson's thesis in *The Wound and the Bow*. Although Wilson referred specifically to writers, his theory is applicable to artists in general. It stems from the Greek legend of the lead-up to the siege of Troy. Philoctetes, an unusually skilled bowman who possessed the arrows of Hercules, had halted with the Greek army at the island of Lemnos on the way to Troy. There he suffered the bite of a serpent at the shrine of Juno whom he had offended. It caused a noisome wound that would not heal. But in the tenth year of the siege when the Greeks had failed to take the city, they sent for Philoctetes hoping that his skill would help them to reduce the Trojans. He returned, and shortly afterwards the city fell, thus ending the war. Wilson's thesis is that the artist is like Philoctetes. We have to accept him whole with all his failings. We cannot have his outstanding skills unadulterated. We have to suffer his disabilities as well, as an integral part of his being. Morris was a real Philoctetes, in his way a skilled archer in his aims. His achievements were never fully recognized and he remains one of the unsung cultural architects of our time, a disseminator of the truth that good physical surroundings and familiarity with good art and design are a vital part of a child's education.

The outbreak of the Spanish War with the army's invasion of the country from north Africa polarized political feeling in Britain. This was especially so in Cambridge where support for the Spanish government was enthusiastic and from where a small number of students and others went to Spain and joined the Republican Army. 'Aid for Spain' became the rallying cry of most left-wing political groups. Marches and demonstrations on Parker's Piece were frequent. They increased when it became known that John Cornford, son of Professor Cornford and his wife Frances Cornford the poet had been killed fighting with the International Brigade, part of the Republican Army. Much of my sparetime activity was spent in attending and helping to organize some of these meetings. There was a sincere desire of people from most sections of the population to help the Republic, very similar to the massive support for Nuclear Disarmament in the Fifties and Sixties. Apart from the argument that a British democracy should help a fellow-democracy threatened by two dictators, many felt, after the open intervention of Hitler and Mussolini in the Spanish war, that the battle-line in Europe was already being drawn and it was incumbent on our government to take an anti-dictator stand. Later, the defeat of the Spanish Republic and the Nazi seizure of Czechoslovakia, following the Chamberlain 'peace in our time' fiasco, induced a feeling of certainty that the protest movements, the demonstrations, the political oratory would not now prevent war. It was only a matter of stage management before the terrible show would begin. Although the first act had not yet been written the actors would soon be confronting one another on the stage, with or without a script.

In the spring of 1939 we took our very young daughter to London to visit Florence's parents. The appearance of trenches in the London parks and open spaces, the increasing numbers of soldiers and airmen in the streets, air-raid wardens with arm bands and steel helmets, the confident military personnel who sensed that at last they were about to do the job they were trained for and were eager to take over, showed that in spite of everything there was a communal will to war; they were all eloquent witnesses that war's juggernaut had already started to roll though war had not formally been declared. It rolled on inexorably, as though it was determined apart from the wills of men and women, a consequence of their apparently unrelated actions and desires that now made violent conflict an inescapable outcome. In the middle of all our wordy arguments about our intentions, about Russia and the dictators, there was already a feeling—hardly conscious at first—that individuals, even groups of individuals, could now decide nothing. Decision had effectively gone out of our hands. Unless a man turned his back on all war and renounced all violent conflict, the individual's power to affect future events had passed. He was now involved in one of the huge irrational movements that encompassed mankind.

I felt this myself and I found, although my conviction remained intact, that the urgency was removed from political activities. I was still an active member of the Communist group and did my job as secretary, but I devoted more time to my writing. I wrote a number of stories at this period and they were published in Robert Herring's *Life and Letters*

*Today*, a magazine that was financed by a lady who called herself Bryher, a writer who was a member of the shipping family of Ellerman. I had also written a verse-play about a mine disaster that I had in mind for a long time. I completed it in time to enter for a B.B.C. (Wales) radio competition that was part of the 1939 National Eisteddfod at Denbigh. At the beginning of August I heard that it had taken the prize and that it would be produced by the B.B.C. 'in due course'. Three weeks or so from hearing this war was declared and the B.B.C. closed down, except for news. I lost my duplicate of the script of the play, and a year or so after the war when I was demobilized I contacted the B.B.C. to see if they had a copy of it. They could not trace it. The verse-play had gone to the bottom without a bubble. A pity, but I am pretty sure that had it survived it would not have set the Taf on fire.

The war started on the first week-end in September when there was an air-raid warning shortly after the declaration, and another one that night or early the following morning. There was no siren and air-raid wardens went round blowing whistles to indicate that an alert was on. There was no action and I believe it was a false alarm. I drew the curtains and looked out. It was bright moonlight and the scene was informed with a nightmare atmosphere as I listened to the shrill whistling and the dream-like reflections of trees and bushes across the road. Just at that moment the whistler came into view. He was a tall man running as though in a panic, his body leaning forward and his head jerking up as he glanced from side to side, all the time blowing vociferously on his whistle. He was not so much alerting the people as inducing fear that would have been no worse if bombs were actually falling. That paradoxically was one of my grimmest memories of the war.

Trains of evacuees now followed one another out of London. A train of mothers and children, young ones and others of school age, deposited a large party in the village of Shelford. I was among those who helped to receive them at the village hall. This was for me one of the most affecting experiences of the war: sixty or so mothers with pre-school children, some with a child in arms as well as a toddler, waiting in a cheerless village hall for well meaning but unpractised people to fill in forms allowing each mother and her child or children to be delivered to a house in the village. Everybody was kind and understanding and the reception they got in the village seemed to be uniformly friendly. Yet the expression on the faces of the mothers after the trauma of not knowing where they were going and waiting in a crowded London station, then travelling a fairly long journey with the children, bewildered by the strangeness of the experience, told the whole story as they waited their turn to be allocated. But there was one irrepressible Cockney woman from the East End, the kind that had never known security and whose daily life was an unending battle against poverty, hardly knowing where the next meal was coming from. She was sitting on the end of the front row: she had a pale, full face with jet black hair. She had one child in her arms and a two-year-old was wandering about in the aisle. She chatted to the woman sitting next to her—with apparent animation as though it was all a new adventure, as indeed it must have been compared with the devastating sameness of the unending pressures at home.

That summer was followed by a very severe winter. Then came the end of the 'phoney war', the German breakthrough and the evacuation of the army from Dunkirk. I have the image of a hot summer afternoon, while playing with Jane in the garden of the bungalow, and a sudden overcast in the south-east. The burning of an oil dump and smoke from the battle drifting over the Channel had sent up a dense cloud that was visible from south Cambridgeshire. A few days later, after a trying day at school, I went for a walk in the evening towards the Gogs. A regiment of Scottish Highlanders evacuated from Dunkirk was on a marching exercise and was coming over the hill and going in the direction of the town. I first heard the plaintive but stirring notes of the pipes before I could see the marching column. On the still evening air, the bagpipes struck up unsuspected chords of feeling that spoke of the battle once fought and battles still to come. A sadness that was saved from being life-denying by a strain of affirmation that was present in the weary but determined faces of the men: this is our lot, this is what we were born to. The sad music seemed to give them strength to endure. The column came over the hill and marched by as I stood on the roadside. Kilted battle-weary men looking straight ahead as though they were enclosed in a discipline that was not evoked by any command but was called up by what they had been through and still had to be faced in the months in the African desert war that was to come.

Later in the summer came the attempts of the Luftwaffe to immobilize the British fighter force by bombing the aerodromes in the south-east, our main defence against the threatening invasion. It was the start of the Battle of Britain. Nearby Duxford had squadrons of Spitfires and it was one of the main targets. One particular Saturday morning there was a dog-fight just overhead. We put the child in her cot which we covered with a thick mattress. We could hear things falling but there were no explosions, only staccato bursts of machine-guns. A German plane was escaping and had dumped its load of incendiary bombs: we heard afterwards that one had fallen in the hedge opposite the bungalow. Jane, who was coming up to eighteen months, enjoyed the excitement and her comment was: 'She-gander!', her version of machine-guns. Yet the incident on a bright summer morning was not as frightening as the air-raid warden's panic running on the first day of the war; and it underscored the truth that fear has no direct relation to actual danger, and even comes after the event in a sudden realization of what might have happened.

The normal programme at the Village College had been suspended. The children were kept in their own villages and shared the school with the juniors who attended in the morning. It meant that one or two masters went to a school and took over in the afternoon. I went with Ernest Foster, the deputy warden, to my own village of Shelford. Later I cycled out to an isolated village, Babraham, near the Gogs. The school was a church school under the aegis of the Adeanes of Babraham Hall, and is now an animal research station. It was very much a close village, that is, it was more or less ruled by the squire. I was there only a week and it was a quiet break with a pleasant class of rural children. There were two sons of the gamekeeper, a keen cricketer who had coached his two sons expertly, and most of the other boys and girls had parents who worked on the estate. It was a deeply rural village which was typical of the previous century and not so unusual in the first half of this one.

While I was there an incident happened that gave me a good insight into the atmosphere of the close village in East Anglia. We were going on peacefully with some lesson or other when suddenly the door opened and in walked a middle-aged man wearing a straw hat and a light linen jacket. He carried a walking stick, and behind him followed a parson. They looked momentarily at the class, paused but without saying anything, turned and went out with as little ceremony as they had come in. It happened so quickly that I brushed the incident off as the sort of occurrence that one could expect in disturbed times. Later I realized, and it was confirmed by the children, that it was a routine, clinical inspection from the 'big house'. The plain rudeness of the interruption was almost certainly due to pique. Probably it was usual for the younger children of the school when it had visitors from the 'big house' to rise to their feet and to remain dutifully standing until told to sit down by their teacher. When they remained sitting the two visitors showed their displeasure by refusing to recognize the new teacher, treating him as part of the furniture that had been imported, without their permission, possibly, into *their* school.

We had two or three London teachers attached to the Sawston staff and their presence evened out the work. There was, too, more interesting conversation in the staff-room and the need to adapt and improvise caused by the crowded school prevented the boredom of a too closely ordered routine. We were, it seemed, far from the war with only occasional fire-watching to do at night. Yet one afternoon, just after dinner, when the children were scattered about the playing field, the war suddenly came to our notice in a dramatic fashion. I was supervising outside during that day. There had been no air-raid warning and the whole school was away from the trenches that had been constructed for us to take cover. I was walking across the cloisters on my way to the library when I heard the spluttering of an aircraft engine. I looked up and saw a German plane, a Dornier, only a couple of hundred feet up. It was losing height after being interrupted on a reconnaissance mission and hit by one of our aircraft or more likely an anti-aircraft gun. It came down on the slopes of the Gogs.

At home we had an evacuee schoolboy from London, a pleasant ten-year-old who fitted into our small household quite smoothly. He was an only child and his mother visited him at week-ends as often as she could—which was a mistake. We noticed that the lad was constantly being disturbed by having to adjust to two 'home' regimes: his old accustomed one and the new one he already adjusted to quite quickly. The tension he felt during and after his mother's visit was considerable. Florence had her hands full with an active, lively child and now the new member of the family. The lad was interested in the baby and would often play with her before she went to bed at night. At the end of October the baby's bedtime roughly coincided with the blackout. This was a nightly exercise; and one was reminded of the importance given to this chore by the real danger of attention from enemy aircraft and by the air-raid wardens who paraded the streets and set a very high standard, especially at this period. If your light showed a mere chink, there would be a loud knocking at the door and an insistent warning that your blackout was not adequate.

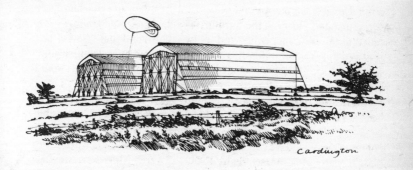

# II · A Blue Uniform

In spite of the war conditions and the knowledge that I would be called up into the services during the coming months, we had settled down to an almost suburban pattern of living. This was rudely disturbed. I was taking a class of boys in physical training one Thursday morning when the warden rushed into the hall: 'Your bungalow is on fire! I've just had a telephone message. Leave the class: I'll run you over in my car.' As I got into the car I asked him about Florence and the child. He said the only message was that the place was ablaze. We could see a column of smoke rising above the houses from about half a mile away, and as we got nearer we saw the fire brigade and a knot of people watching. Florence and Jane were safe and were in the house of a neighbour. Florence was slightly burned about the face. John, the evacuee, was still at school and knew nothing about the fire. It had started in the room where there were the books and manuscripts, which Florence tried to rescue. The first thing to do was to take Florence to hospital to have her face dressed. It was only superficially burned. We spent that night with immediate neighbours and afterwards went to friends who had been putting up civil defence workers to give them a break from the almost continuous bombing of the city. They volunteered to take us in until we could find somewhere to live. As I took Florence to the hospital the thought struck me: 'Did I renew my insurance cover?' I could not recall doing so. I had an irrational reaction against all insurance, especially life insurance; and I had insured the bungalow against fire more to escape the attentions of the insurance agent than anything else. He visited us after Florence's mother had put an announcement of Jane's birth in *The Friend*, and he wanted us to take out an endowment for her. Not to send him away empty-handed I insured the furniture and the household goods. Now I called at the insurance office and to my relief found that I had in fact renewed the premium. But the relief was tempered by realizing that the sum I would get, owing to the rapidly rising prices of the past year, would hardly enable us to refurnish the kitchen.

But neither of us was much put out by the fire, strangely enough, at least not at the time. It was like a sudden death: it was almost impossible to take in. Besides, the wartime atmosphere made loss of property a common event, and we could hardly feel sorry for ourselves when many people were in a worse plight than we were. Moreover, we had socialized our bad luck, and friends and near-strangers were ready to extend their sympathy; their expression of concern was a tremendous help in stopping us from brooding on it. The publicity, being in the public eye, satisfied our vanity too and diverted our attention from the actual loss. Although I knew unconsciously that the fire would burn in our minds for many years to come, it was not as catastrophic in its effect as it appeared at the time. In fact it became one of the factors that effectively changed our lives. The remark of a Cambridgeshire countryman, one of our neighbours, later struck me as fitting our experience: 'Fire, it's a good servant but a right bad maaster.' It certainly played a part in arranging our destiny for the next few years and prevented us from following a suburban course of life that neither of us would have been happy with. Yet the temper of the time was sympathetic to misfortune and this it was, with the reminder that upheavals and loss of home were almost part of the common lot, that prevented us from feeling that we were a family marked out for misfortune.

Few households in the Cambridge area remained the same. The town had a big accession of civil servants forming part of a ministry. Then there were the children who were evacuated; and in the town and country there were troops billeted for special courses in the area. Railwaymen, for instance, who were in the army and had been sent for special training for the time when they would be needed in France. We were lucky to find somewhere to live with friends who worked in Cambridge. They lived a couple of miles from Sawston and we stayed with them a few weeks, when we got rooms in the house of a colleague at the village college. He had just been called up and was glad to have someone to live with his wife who was expecting a baby. I was unable to do any writing at this time because all my writing material had gone, including my typewriter. But I had a few proofs to correct and this did a lot to keep up my morale and keep my ultimate purpose in mind.

Before the war started I had been very impressed by the writings of a Scot, J. Leslie Mitchell, who also wrote under the name of Lewis Grassic Gibbon. He was a friend of Hugh MacDiarmid, the Scottish poet who wrote in Lallans. Mitchell, in addition to factual books, wrote *A Scottish Quair*, a series of novels of which *Sunset Song* was the first. He used the Scottish dialect of the north-east coastal area and it was just as effective for his purpose in prose as it was in verse. On first reading his novels just before the war, I was struck by the suitability of the language for the telling of a tale about Scottish farm life; and I decided to use the words and the rhythms of the demotic English that was spoken in the south Wales valleys, sprinkled as it was with the literal translation of idioms from the Welsh and even directly borrowed Welsh expressions, to hammer out a vehicle for a group of mining valley stories.

But my mind at this time was almost completely on solving the question of where the family would go when I was called up. A great deal of time was spent in the summer attempting to get somewhere for them to live as we could not stay in our present position indefinitely. It was soon apparent that calling on the Cambridge house agents hoping to get a place to live was like looking for field-daisies in the dead of winter. What made it more urgent was that Florence was going to have another baby, something that was planned before the fire. We agonized over this for weeks, and we eventually decided that, if they were agreeable, Florence and the children should go to live with her parents in Enfield, north London. This was a drastic remedy as they would be moving into the bombing zone. Yet the times were such that few could indulge in the nice balancing of risks. Nowhere was absolutely safe. Where we were at the time, theoretically in the country, was not immune from attack. Enfield, at least before the end of the war and the buzz-bombs and rockets, remained fairly safe. In favour of the move was the fact that Florence's mother could help her with the children. Jane was at the stage when she invented little girls as playmates: one was Elsie Marley, an entirely fictitious character, and she would inform us that Elsie Marley had gone to Cambridge. At night she would say: 'Go to sleep now, Elsie Marley.' A few days later her friend was Seety Seity; and she would spend a lot of time playing with her.

Our second child, Matthew, was born almost three months before we left Cambridgeshire. There were now three babies in the small house and it was like a baby farm. When the time came for us to leave, it was a relief for all four parents. We did not know what the future would hold but the unknown was preferable to the reality we were then experiencing. Apart from the wrench of a new start I recall feeling as we left that it was in a way providential as one of us would have cracked during the following winter.

We had little luggage. The main item was a rather large perambulator in which we bundled our belongings, and packed it in the guard's van for Liverpool Street. We travelled the day before I was due to report at the R.A.F. reception centre. Once again I was coming to London at a critical point as though the capital was the real governor, the lodestone of my cursus. This time, however, I was not to stay for long. We went from Liverpool Street by suburban train to the home of Florence's parents and I spent the night with them before taking an early train from St Pancras for Bedford. There R.A.F. lorries met the many civilians who had travelled on the London train independently; and immediately we came together under the orders of hardboiled N.C.Os who got us to Cardington. Although we had not yet reached the camp, already we were transformed men, glancing at our neighbours to see how they were taking the changed status, of being told what to do, and acting without question. We shortly came to an airfield with huge, surrealist hangars built in the inter-war years to house airships. The hangars, surrounded by workshops and huts, dominated the scene like nightmare monsters, and gave an air of unreality to the hundreds of civilians who were being led to various buildings about them, knowing only vaguely why they were being marched about.

We were in the camp three days, the longest days I can remember: being sworn in, kitted out with our uniform, trying it on and wondering at the transformation in the other nineteen men in the hut, knowing that you also were equally changed. Boys of eighteen and young and middle-aged men of all occupations with their status and social gradations were now in a limbo, a kind of blue-grey melting-pot. A short man wearing a service jersey that was too big for him paced about his bed making a list of his gear: he pondered over his piece of paper and, after finishing it and seeming satisfied, he placed the pencil behind his ear as he had been doing for twenty years in the shop where he had been an assistant. Another red-faced Londoner had confided to someone that he had been a taxi driver and he was loudly greeted in the hut the couple of days we were there by the raucous cry of 'taxi'. Each man during those long days of metamorphosis was groping for his identity. The bawling and shoutings of the N.C.Os teaching the recruits to form in squads and perform the elementary drills, the quick-demanded response to the barked out word of command, the sarcasms that fell on the head of someone who had botched a movement, were all part of the transforming of an individual into the passive member of a group under orders.

We had packed our civilian clothes and sent them home: like our true identities they had gone into indefinite storage. We were up very early next day, parading in bright moonlight, We were in long ranks, three or four hundred men altogether. We then learned our first lesson, obviously intended, in waiting patiently in ranks. We were in the command of a warrant officer who to fill in time gave us a longish harangue about security. We were just about to entrain but we did not know where we were going. Now that we were in the R.A.F. it was necessary to be silent about all matters relating to it. Careless talk costs lives. After waiting still longer, with glimpses of light behind the huts, a grey dawn was spread over the camp. A high-ranking officer now appeared with his deputy. The warrant officer, repeated his homily about security to ensure that the higher officer had heard that his orders were carried out. The officer, after a brief few words of his own, handed back the command to the W.O., and at his order, 'In column of route—quick march', we were on our way to the anonymous train waiting in the siding. After hours of being shunted about nameless stations in order to miss London, we arrived on the south coast in the mid-afternoon. 'It's Bournemouth,' someone said. 'I'm sure of it. I've been there!' We marched to a district to the west of the town and were allotted civilian digs in groups of two or three. Our lodgings were a half-mile from a district of large middle-class houses one of which had been converted into a flight office. Here in the affluent suburban rows we did most of our drilling, broken by occasional visits which we enjoyed to the local recreation ground, or field-training on the moors where we did manoeuvres. These respectable avenues were our main base until Christmas: we were shunted there chiefly to waste time, which we improved by watching elderly matrons parade their dogs. After long observation, the scene was summed up succinctly by a Cockney in our squad: 'All fur coats and dog shit.'

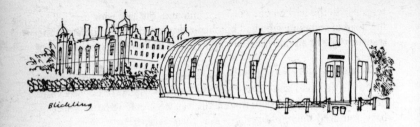

Blickling

# 12 · A Taste of Peace

For the next four and a half years I was in blue uniform—a colour I was never partial to. After the initial training we were dispatched, according to the trade we had chosen, to various training schools up and down the country. When I joined up at Cambridge the officer in charge told me that they badly needed men who had the capacity to absorb an intensive course of technical training within a short time. The service was short of wireless mechanics who were capable of servicing aircraft and ground equipment and keeping them in repair. I had no ambitions as far as the R.A.F. was concerned, and I did not want to enrol as a physical education officer for which I had some qualifications. I wanted a change and was ready to accept the suggestion of a technical course. This meant that writing would have to go into cold storage for the duration of the course, if not of the war. For eight months we were put through an intensive course in electrical and radio theory that kept me extended. I had given up mathematics and science at 'O' level, and now we older men had to keep up with eighteen-year-olds who had just finished school. We attended two courses in technical colleges in London and Lancashire. It was hard work and not an easy experience to live through, but I recognized it as a good corrective: it gave me a greater insight and appreciation of science; and again, a recognition that men who had no particular success in formal education at school were able to hold their own with so-called trained academics. On qualifying I was posted to a coastal command squadron in Norfolk.

During this period I was able to visit the family fairly frequently. When I was at the technical college in the London area, I used to spend the week-ends with them, and then when I was in Lancashire I got Florence to post me a civilian suit. When we had a week-end off I was able to absent myself, returning to my civilian berth early on Monday morning after coming off the London night train. Paradoxically, I found it more disturbing to see the family every week than when I was absent for more than three months. The living in two environments made me more restless and less inured to the unnatural service life. I found that this was the experience of many servicemen who were posted near their homes. One thing I noticed on my return to 'school': I found that invariably I made for the front desk but not because I wanted to push myself forward. It dawned on me gradually that the reason for this was that I could hear better. I refused to admit to myself that I was becoming hard of hearing, as the euphemism goes. At my medical examination on entry into the service I mentioned to the doctor, an affable Scot, that I appeared to be slightly deaf in my right ear. He tested it, assured me that there was nothing to worry about and passed me A1. During the months of instruction my hearing appeared to deteriorate; but in the late summer of that year I discovered that it was noticeably defective. I was posted to Horsham St Faith in Norwich, but was sent immediately to a satellite aerodrome at Oulton. The squadron was billeted at Blickling Hall, now the outstanding National Trust house a couple of miles away. I was directed to a hut of 'riggers', tradesmen who worked on the aircraft frame, until I was able to get a bed in my own section of signals. I arrived about six o'clock when most of the men were changing or resting after tea. I placed my kitbag down and started unpacking. There was a sudden silence in the drone of the conversation: I became aware of it and turned round. I found that the men in the opposite beds to mine were looking at me questioningly. One of them had spoken to me and I had not heard. I discovered later that I had a type of deafness that enabled me to hear a conversation if there was already a background of noise, whereas during a silence I was unable to hear a noise of identical level.

After the initial shock I became self-conscious about my condition and when a little later I visited the M.O. to have a piece of iron filing removed from my eye I asked him to test my hearing. He found that it was defective and arranged for me to visit the group hospital at Ely. The consultant diagnosed a condition called otosclerosis, which he said was probably hereditary. He asked me what my job was in the R.A.F. and whether my indifferent hearing interfered with it. I told him I thought I could do the job; and with that he downgraded me to medical category C. That meant the rest of my service was United Kingdom only, home service with no overseas posting. Thinking of the future, I explained that I was a schoolteacher and asked him what the prognosis of the complaint was. He advised me to look for another job on release from service, before my hearing went much worse. Recently a friend who is an E.N.T. consultant told me that there is a misconception about the name of this condition of the ear. The word was coined from two Greek words which mean 'hardening of the ear', implying that the little bones or ossicles of the inner ear were thought to have become anchylosed, whereas the bones in fact become softened. This is now only of philological interest to me, but it confirms that the ear is a very tricky piece of bodily apparatus.

Although the restriction of my service to home postings was an unlooked-for blessing from the standpoint of the family and, indeed, of myself, at first I was very much put down by the regrading. I was now categorized as being abnormal and this was an assault on my precious self-esteem. I was no longer wholly sound: I probably had some other imperfections but I was ignorant of them and therefore I could continue safely with the illusion of being fit. Through the realization of my deafness I insensibly became more introspective, uncertain in situations that people ordinarily sailed through unself-consciously, retreating from meeting people, as that would show my weakness—that is, rationalizing to prevent the deafness being exposed unnecessarily. Before the war, for example, I was very fond of the theatre; after I was demobilized I persuaded myself I was no longer interested in the theatre (this was tantamount to saying I was no longer interested in life) when the real truth was that I could not hear properly, and going to the theatre was a strain. When later on I got an adequate hearing-aid, I enjoyed the theatre as much as I had ever done. I remember reading somewhere that when Goya, the Spanish painter, went deaf his work took a new direction, as though his lack of hearing had sent him into himself and forced him to use his eyes even more, thus enabling him to see with deeper insight, to notice the darker side of the world. It is certain that deafness alters one's centre of awareness, and while I cannot vouch for concentrating on the gloomier side of life, as I was not exactly a Candide to start with, I am more conscious of people's feelings and able to project more into their possible difficulties. I believe, though, that my visual sense improved. I missed little that came through the eye, and I was able to identify immediately strangers with whom I had only come into casual contact, placing them exactly in the setting of my first sighting. I developed, quite unconsciously, an acute memory for faces; and I have more than once surprised Florence by identifying by his face a person who was hardly known to us, so that she has often told me that I should have been a detective. If I had, I would probably have been a public menace.

One thing hardness of hearing breeds inevitably is bodily tensions. I became keyed up to catch every syllable and consequently became so tense that what hearing I had left became impeded by this increase of tension. On parade the commands were usually very loud and there was rarely any difficulty: if there was, I managed to get away with it through reacting a fraction of a second after the others. As I normally worked in aircraft, inspecting and servicing them on the ground, there were in ordinary circumstances no panic occasions and I was able to get along on an even tenor. On one aerodrome, I worked for a short while in station headquarters instead of my usual work with an operational squadron. One of the jobs was on nightwatch at the transmitter station situated in the middle of a field a mile or so from the aerodrome. It was necessary to have a mechanic at the transmitter to invigilate its performance by means of the various dials, and to adjust the controls to give the correct readings. The duty officer at the 'drome was in touch with the transmitter cabin by telephone. It was difficult to get much sleep at first as every time the operator keyed her message in morse-code back at the 'drome the relays in the transmitter would chatter in time with the keying. I woke periodically during the night to check the reading, but my main worry was that I should turn over during the night on my good ear while asleep and not hear the telephone. Fortunately, the telephone never rang while I was on watch, and shortly afterwards I went back to the squadron and to my usual work. Little situations like this exercised me out of all proportion, for although they were routine, they were minor links in a long chain whose breakage would be disastrous.

The squadron I had joined was in coastal command and for a couple of years we were up and down the east coast like a shoal of herring. I was at various times in coastal stations from the south coast to the Orkneys—Norfolk, Lincolnshire, north Yorkshire, east Fife, working on Beaufighters, Wellingtons, Wellesleys, Hudsons and, at the later stages of the war, Liberators and Flying Fortresses. I spent a long time in Scotland after D–Day, first at Turnberry on the site of the converted golf course, and later at Leuchars in sight of another golf course in St Andrews.

I felt at home in Scotland. In an almost indefinable way I was relaxed and outgoing with the Scots as, after the war, I was with the Irish. It convinced me, in spite of the blether written about the Celtic fringes, that after all there was something real in a Celtic affinity. It is nothing mysterious, not necessarily caused by race or blood-relatedness but, in essence, it is due to a similar experience of what in its essentials is an identical folklife over long centuries. The Celtic peoples had got their living from the soil through their animals who grazed on it. This, too, even among the English, differentiates the north of England from the southern counties and generates the kind of separatist, local conscious-ness that distinguishes the north from the south. The people of the south and, especially of East Anglia, were from their beginnings arable farmers and their life followed the inbred rhythm of the farming that had conditioned them for centuries.

A fairly long stay on the west coast of Scotland convinced me also of the truth, in the purely physical sense, of the loosely used phrase 'Celtic twilight'. There is a world of difference between evening on the east and west coast, and especially an evening where the sun sets in view of the Scottish islands. During the war air-crew flying to the Continent sometimes described to me the beauty of the sun rising out of the North Sea and casting its myriad shades of light over the water. But it has not been celebrated like the setting of the sun on the west coasts of Britain. Perhaps one of the reasons for this is that most people are asleep, except sailors and fishermen, and do not see the sun's rising. In the moisture-laden air of a still evening on the west coast of Scotland, the sunsets are often like a sight behind a curtain lifted by the gods: the golden lane across the water, the stillness of the air and the diffusion of a golden-tinged light reflected on a rocky coastline, the strange illusion of islands and headlands lying *out* of the water but separate and resting lightly or even floating upon it. Ailsa Craig, the bluff rock off the coast, the sanctuary of the gannets, the Mull of Kintyre, the remote islands, and the smooth plane of the light-reflecting sea made a scene that stays and reappears in the mind interminably, bringing a gift of perpetual renewal.

It was on such an evening as this that I had a day off from the aerodrome and went by camp bus to the town of Ayr, returning by an ordinary service bus in the mid-evening. The bus went on to the town of Govan and dropped me on the main road, to walk down the hill to the camp that was about a mile away on a gentle descent. A young girl got off the bus at the same time. She wore W.A.A.F. uniform and we walked down to the camp together. She was a wireless operator in the station headquarters—in signals, the same trade as I was in. She came from the Isle of Lewis, and had the dark colouring of the people of the islands and a pensive air, the inwardness that marks off some of the women of the west coast and the islands. As soon as we came in sight of the sea, we saw a beautiful sunset; stretched out below us was the whole scene even more spectacular than it appeared from the shore. We stopped for a moment or two and stood in silence. Then we walked on, admiring the scene spread out below us. Then she said quietly as though communing with herself and not addressing a remark to me: 'And I've promised to marry an Englishman!' A strange, incongruous remark uttered more in a tone of puzzlement than with any tinge of regret that made me wonder whether she had on impulse given word to a thought that had suddenly crossed her mind. I hesitated, therefore, to intrude on her full consciousness by letting her know that I had heard. At last, I broke the rather embarrassing silence by asking her whether he was someone on the present camp. She told me she was to marry a sergeant in our section headquarters. I knew him only by sight as my job was at the dispersal unit, a squadron right on the lip of the sea. I could see that the girl was troubled by something yet it was not my role to press her further to tell me her doubts. I was a stranger and would probably not see her again in a dispersed camp—as actually happened. Yet I often wondered whether her uncensored remark and her implied doubts about marrying the Englishman were triggered off by the scene below us: if she married her Englishman she would probably follow him to his home in the south; she would move to a different scene and she would get none of the sustenance that was then coming to us from the view of the straits below and the splendour of the islands on the horizon beyond.

I gained a real lift of spirit from my stay in the west of Scotland—as I had a year or so before from a brief stay in treeless Orkney. We flew up from North Coates in Lincolnshire on a detachment of four or five Beaufighters, to co-operate with the Fleet that was at Scapa Flow. The plan was for a three or four days' exercise. The pilot of my plane was an Irishman and the observer was a young student from University College, Swansea. As a passenger, I sat in the well behind the pilot. The flight was my first: it was a bright April day and was enjoyable, particularly the approach to Orkney across the Pentland Firth. We landed on the Mainland at Grimster, a satellite of Kirkwall, in late afternoon, ready for starting the exercise next morning. The dawn, however, broke with mist and rain, which persisted and made flying impossible. On the first day we were released from duty as the mist continued, and I and a Suffolk man who was with me went into a café where we had an 'unrationed' meal in the town of Kirkwall. I found out later that Grimster was quite near the Garth, the farm where the poet

Edwin Muir lived and which he describes in *An Autobiography*. The aerodrome was on a boggy apron of land right at the edge of the sea, and fitted in with Muir's description of the land as poor: it constantly needed draining as we found out as soon as we landed. One of the Beaufighters, a heavy, well armoured machine, got bogged down in a kind of open drain as we were taxi-ing around to a dispersal site; and it had to be left behind as the aerodrome did not have a crane to lift it.

The mist persisted for three days and as there was no flying we drifted out of camp to explore some of the countryside. One of the camp regulars suggested that we call at the farm of a crofter that was just half a mile or so on the hill from where our huts were sited. We were welcomed by the crofter and his wife as old friends; and they sold each of us a dozen eggs, which were almost as rare as gold at that time of rationing. The crofter had a job on the aerodrome, and he and his wife were probably better off than they had ever been for, as I read in Edwin Muir's book, the land was hungry, demanding constant and unremitting toil to win a bare subsistence. The wife had a beautiful speaking voice and spoke an attractive dialect. I remember a word she used, 'forby', a common word in Lallans, meaning 'besides'. They showed us Eric Linklater's house on a headland that was visible from the hill. He was one of Orkney's best-known sons and during the previous decade had written a book called *Juan In America* that brought him fame. I came across the name of Linklater again in 1963 when I again flew up to Thurso, within sight of Orkney, to meet Norman Halkett, the son of an Aberdeenshire farmer who was a member of the Society of the Horseman's Word, a secret society of Scottish horsemen that I had come to hear about. He mentioned that he had once worked in Orkney and was at one time convener of the Orkney branch of the society. He told me, as an example of its underground existence, that Linklater had stated in one of his books that the Horseman's Word and the society were a myth—at the very time when an active member of the society was living within a stone's throw of Linklater's door.

While I was at Turnberry, I used to visit Glasgow on a day off duty. I made an attempt to meet Hugh MacDiarmid who was living in Glasgow and working at a wartime job in a factory. He worked unusual hours on shift work and as I could get away from the camp only rarely I failed to see him. He stayed after the war at Onllwyn in the Neath valley with Dafydd Aubrey and his wife Mair but I again missed the chance of meeting him. He was a first-class poet who will long outlive his more fashionable contemporaries. His poems, *A Drunk Man Looks at the*

*Thistle* and *Island Funeral*, and many of his lyrics, show his true stature. At Turnberry, too, I was in Burns country and I was near many of the places where he had lived. I also visited Kirkoswald where he was born, Ayr and Kilmarnock where his first book of poems was printed. I stayed at Ballochmyle House, a wartime hospital where my hearing was being investigated. The hospital was surrounded by wooded grounds, just above the village of Mauchline. An arbour in the grounds was pointed out to us as the place where Burns sat with the *Lass of Ballochmyle*, the subject of one of his poems.

In these months of the winter 1943 and spring of the following year, I was stimulated by being in tune with the natural scene to write a great deal. Whenever I could, I would get away to the hut that the education officer allowed me to use out of hours. I occasionally took an evening off to cycle around the countryside with a couple of the men in my section. The looming shadow of the post-war years was beginning to trouble me. I had gone deafer as the consultant had forecast, and it would only be shelving the problem to go back to my old job. It was partly this concern that caused a new burst of writing. I had already started a manuscript, an autobiographical fiction of my earlier years in the valley, during my stay in the Lincolnshire aerodrome. I wrote in NAAFI rest-rooms, in bars, and under hedges in the summer when it was fine. Many of the scripts were stories that were published in service compilations: *Bugle Blast*, *First Eighteen*, and magazines like *Lilliput* and *Life and Letters Today* whose editor Robert Herring was a constant encouragement.

I also wrote some verse at Turnberry. In the winter the straits and the islands were transformed. One of them stood out like a tall, commanding Soracte. Along with a Plymouth man who shared our hut I went into the grounds of Culzean Castle, the home of the Marquess of Ailsa. He had given permission to servicemen to walk in the grounds. One evening we met his wife, a middle-aged lady wearing a black cloak. She stopped and talked with us, repeating that men from the R.A.F. camp were very welcome: if, however, we came across a gold watch she had lost on one of her strolls, she would be obliged if we returned it to her. After the war the castle and its grounds were given as a gift to General Eisenhower for his war service, but I doubt whether he used it much. Apart from its romantic situation, it must have been a cold, rather forbidding place to live in—stone-built, right on the edge of the cliff and very secure, but hardly the kind of place to relax in.

The natural scene was a constant source of interest. We waited on the dunes for the planes to return from their exercises over the straits and the islands. On rare, still days we could see outlines of further islands to the west. On other days we watched the gannets—Ailsa Craig was their breeding place—flying low over the water, their wings for a split second as low as the ears of a spaniel dog. Then they would lift themselves into the air and from the height of a couple of hundred feet fold their wings and drop like a plummet into the burnished steel of still sea. They sometimes surfaced with a fish between their beaks, and striking the water with their webbed feet, would fly off towards their breeding place. The fishermen told us that it was possible to gauge the depth the shoals of fish were lying at from the angle of the gannets' dive. A shallow dive revealed that the fish were just below the surface, but when the birds ascended to a fair height and descended suddenly like deadly white arrows, the shoals were lying deep in the water of the bay.

The rock of Ailsa Craig and the waters of the bay towards the village of Maidens and beyond had many faces. There were days when a mist hid the scene altogether; others when a storm would cause the sea to beat against the shore of the headlands and the waves to break high over the rocky coast. Occasionally, Ailsa Craig would appear to be floating in the air, the sea mist making its base invisible. Yet it could change very quickly when the sun shone through the clouds and cast broad shadows on the sea. The dark patches became a deep purple, suffused by a pinkish orange glow especially round the edges. Across the bay towards the evening I have seen a thin orange sun-lane with shimmering cross-lines caused by the ripples of the sea, making the reflection appear like a Chinese lantern. The isles of exile became more secret and remote as the light faded, and numbers of big birds, probably cormorants flew low over the water with definite purpose, making for their breeding place.

The scene had a never-ending variety and appeal, yet it had another hidden facet that was only revealed after I had been in the station for a couple of months. A Beaufighter coming to land on the cross runway that ran at right angles to the bay suddenly stalled as one of its engines cut a hundred yards or so out. It was a heavy-armoured plane and its nose went down immediately and it crashed into the water. It was reported at the time that the pilot released his safety-harness just before the plane's impact with the water and he was dashed against the thickened perspex. This incident caused other accidents that had happened during the last two or three years to surface and be recounted. It was not an 'operational' aerodrome but was used chiefly for training aircrews; this accident made me ponder the sea and look at it in a new light. On a showery day, when the clouds were 'nine-tenths' and the water a resentful grey, it was easy to imagine the disasters that came up and were recounted by the old-stagers. The one most often recalled happened in the early years of the war. Three Wellington bombers went out on an 'O.F.E.'—an Operational Flying Exercise. It was a moonlit night and the planes set off over the clear, still waters of the bay, simulating a low level approach and flying close to the water. They were flying line-astern (Indian file). The leader misjudged and hit the water and went down: the others, seeing his navigation lights that still burned momentarily, followed on his tail, and went straight in after him. Aircrews flying on roughly the same course a few years later while we were on the aerodrome reported that in certain lights they could distinguish the shapes of the three aircraft lying deep in the clear waters of the strait, like huge stranded fish. It made us ponder the green-skulled aircrews lying unmarked and forgotten in the depths of the cold waters.

Although my stay at this station was the nearest I approached to contentment in the morass of service life, I was not as lucky on other postings; and I often felt I should have gone berserk were it not for my writing. This had a decidedly therapeutic effect and gave me a strong foothold when I felt that I was descending into the depths. Separated from Florence and the children and plagued by the inescapable guilt that while I was in the north and in comparative safety they were under risk, it was impossible to be really content in such a position, and to ease my conscience I used to try and write to them on most days. On home service we were very lucky to be in constant touch with the family and to be able to see them at not too long intervals. Letters were delivered and received; and it was possible to go on leave to London from Scotland easily; and I had great admiration for the sterling job the railwaymen did during the war and for the unsung postmen who delivered the letters that were the serving man's lifeline.

I went home on leave from Scotland and spent a quiet time with Florence and the two children. They were both attending a local school where Florence herself had gone back to teaching. The family were sleeping in a Morrison shelter downstairs in the living-room. It was a metal case that during the day was covered with a cloth and served as a kind of table. At this time, in 1944, the Second Front had just opened and there was no fear of attacks. During the whole time I was home there was little enemy activity over the south-east. We took the children to a fête and horse show in Enfield, and I was amazed by the normality of the event, and the reappearance of pre-war types who seemed suddenly and incongruously to emerge, so that for a bright, sunny afternoon the war, as it were, had receded and we were back in what were, in this area, the halcyon days of the Thirties. Less than a year later, with the start of the last of Hitler's desperate attacks on London with the buzz-bombs and the V2 rockets, no part of south-east England was safe. A V2 fell a couple of streets away from where the family was staying, but it did little damage and no one was hurt. During the children's early years, their illnesses loomed larger than any war danger, but they were growing up healthily on the whole, and we were never in dire anxiety about them.

I returned to camp to find I had been posted to another station, but my disappointment was tempered by the fact that I was still to be in Scotland. I was going to a squadron of Liberators, the American four-engined planes which were engaged in anti-submarine patrol along the coasts of northern Europe. The station was on the east coast at Leuchars, near Dundee. It overlooked St Andrew's, the university town, and the golf course was just across the water from the 'drome. Leuchars was an important operational station, especially at this stage of the war in Europe. The station included also a Czech squadron. There were not many Poles at this particular period. They appeared to be farther south, in Edinburgh, near which there were fighter squadrons. Edinburgh had a cosmopolitan atmosphere about it, especially when the Americans were added to the mix. There was also a Norwegian army unit stationed on the east coast; and there was a direct link from Sweden (which was neutral) to Leuchars. A Hudson plane did the trip to Sweden and back regularly.

After being a week at Leuchars I realized I was right in the middle of the war again. It was nearing its end and the anti-submarine activity in the Channel and the North Sea stepped up tremendously. The planes were sinking more submarines than before, possibly because the traffic to and from their bases had increased owing to the crisis. Work was much harder. Apart from the squadron's scale of operations there was more signals equipment on the big planes we had to service. Yet it was usually possible to get a day off a week and get a break from camp routine. How different the east coast was from the west. Only rarely could one see a tinge of colour in the sea. It was a uniform grey, and the greyness appeared to permeate the towns and the villages along the coast, constructed as they were of grey granite. St Andrews is a fine centre with its attractive university buildings and the houses with their corby or crow-step gables. But it has a cold air, and even on a sunny summer's day only the very hardy ventured into the water—at least in the summer of 1945. We were more fortunate at Turnberry where under the aegis of the Gulf Stream we bathed regularly during the previous summer. But what a contrast St Andrews was to Dundee. The university town was orderly and circumspect, having a middle-class air about it. From a diary I kept at the time, my first visit rather coloured the town of Dundee for me. I was walking in Overgate but was stopped by a crowd that was fluctuating from side to side of the narrow street. Two women were fighting. One went down and was helped up by a coloured soldier. The other woman skirting the inside of the crowd went in again. A flurry of women in shawls came together and one of them said: 'They nigh killed yon lassie last night!' There was a throwing up of first-floor windows in the street and three or four women leaned out of the windows—'hinging oot'—and shouted encouragement to both of the combatants. The police soon came along and separated the women and dispersed the crowd, while the women who were 'hanging out' looked down as though they were goddesses above mortal strife, and made inaudible comments, nodding their heads sagely at one another all the while. My next visit to Dundee balanced my rather biased first impression. I went with a few members of the signals section to a concert in the Caird Hall, given by the Hallé Orchestra, of Elgar's rendering of an old Welsh tune and Brahms's First Symphony. A programme note said: 'This is music for the soul.' In my mood at the time, I would have preferred it to be solely for the ear.

The pressure of work was such that even if we had no outside news it was clear that a crisis had been reached. The war was quickly coming to an end but there was a defensive wariness of any emotion. The fighting itself was so remote to us that although we could give the ending a full intellectual assent, and would be glad that it was all over, we knew that we could not be personally affected by the armistice. Our position would not change appreciably and demobilization would not come, so I estimated, for another six months. What would happen in the meantime? Florence was about to have another child and had recently gone to a maternity home in Oxfordshire. As the month of April wore on the work increased, and some days we were on duty for fourteen hours on aircraft we were not totally familiar with. The winter had been very severe and we were immured in a large, claustrophobic hangar for days at a time, servicing the planes that were wheeled out relentlessly as they were completed, for fresh ones to come in as soon as they had finished their quota of flying time and were due for inspection. Then on 6 May I noted: 'All German resistance seems to have broken down. It is probable that Hitler has already killed himself. Western Europe has surrendered—all except Norway. Our Liberators are still bombing convoys in the Skaggerak and the Baltic but it is likely that the Germans in Norway will surrender very shortly. This evening's six o'clock news says that V Day will be announced before next Thursday. There is something artificial in "this will be announced". Churchill is to speak on Thursday. This day has been so long anticipated that now it is almost here we are too jaded to have any feelings about it. Most of the joyous feeling will perhaps be in retrospect.' On 7 May I wrote:

> We heard that 206 Squadron [our squadron] had been recalled from 'Ops' [Operations]. Norway has surrendered. Went to sleep after tea. Arthur Durham [a rigger] woke me up to tell me there had been a break-in message on the wireless: VE day will be tomorrow. Churchill will speak at 3 o'clock, 8 May, VE day. If only we could experience the right emotions at the right time.' A telegram from Florence this morning: 'A daughter [Mary] born yesterday.'

After the war in Europe had finished events quickened. The squadron had orders to move south to Oakington, a few miles from Cambridge. Being so near would give me a chance to look about for a house in the town. Getting a house for the family was even as important as getting a job; perhaps more so. We had both been happy in the Cambridge area and wanted to go back to it. The squadron moved south on the last day of July. In less than a week the first atomic bomb was dropped on Hiroshima, followed by the bombing of Nagasaki. The war in the Far East ended immediately. The order then came through to convert the huge Liberators to transport planes. They ripped out the bomb equipment from the bays and equipped them to give seats for the prisoners of war who were to be repatriated from the Far East. I wrote in my diary at the time: 'The papers say a new era in world history has started. Mars is the presiding deity. They say that atomic energy is already almost controllable for industrial purposes and that it will cause a greater revolution than the harnessing of steam at the beginning of the industrial era. I tell myself that there may be a new era beginning. Potentially, I suppose, it could be a new millennium. Yet, as I see it now, international control of armaments will become a real vital and practical necessity; not merely a concession to the thinkers and idealists and a minority of the more enlightened, practical men. J. B. S. Haldane says the new discoveries will render the railways obsolete in thirty years.'

As the ex-prisoners were ferried back from the East we became busier than when the squadron was operational; but it was more satisfying to be doing something useful. We did not see many of the repatriated men. They were whisked away in conveyances straight off the tarmac after the planes had taxied in. What we did see later was the aircrew with bundles of carpets that they had bought in Bombay, one of the stages on the way back, piling them straight into taxis that were taking them to Cambridge.

I heard before Christmas that I would be demobilized in February. But before this happened I had my first serious rift with authority since I had been in the Air Force. Like most conscripts, now that the war was over, I wanted to be out and was fretting at the delay. Yet an order that came through from group headquarters more than tried my patience. I was ordered to proceed on a highly technical course, lasting a month or so, to Uxbridge, one of the R.A.F.'s *templa arcanorum*. I decided I was not going. First I explained to our flight sergeant, a very decent chap, that I was about to be demobilized within a couple of months. He referred me to the station signals officer who told me it was an order and I would have to go. I tried to get him to cancel the posting. But he was adamant and said it was a definite posting. I then informed him that I would make a request to see the station commander. It was my right and he could not refuse. Demanding to see a senior officer after I had been given an order was rather a long shot and had little hope of success. But I had seen the station commander at one of the parades; and he did not look like the typical brass-hat: he had the look of an intelligent man. And I was willing to take a chance. I was taken before him by the signals officer and I stated my case: I was shortly to be demobilized, and if I went on the proposed course it would be a waste of service money, as I would not be in the R.A.F. long enough to use the knowledge I had gained on this particular course. The group captain found it a reasonable argument. It would be unprofitable from the R.A.F.'s standpoint, and he turned to the signals officer with the question: 'Don't you think so?' His answer was a lame one: 'I appreciate Evans's case.'

Release from the R.A.F. came in February. It would be difficult to change my job at this stage, especially as we had no house of our own. Although it was not a long-term solution if I went back to my job in Sawston, I would be in the area and surely I could find somewhere once I was living there. At the end of my demobilization leave, I went back to my old job, staying during the week with friends at Shelford. I travelled up on the same train to London as I had when I was in the R.A.F. at Oakington. The failure to be together was a great disappointment to both of us. I realized after being in my old job for a week or so that I would not find a house in the Cambridge area. And I decided to find a job teaching near the family. This was made imperative by the news that Florence was going to have another baby. I got a job in a London school that was within cycling distance of where the family lived. The new school made me aware of how pleasant conditions were at Sawston. It was a three-storey barracks of a school, a bleak nineteenth-century learning-factory that I reacted against violently. For most of my time there I was teaching English, having given up physical education.

Duxford

*Blaxhall*

## 13 · *Suffolk and a Fresh Start*

The immediate post-war years were a difficult period for most people including those who had just been demobilized and were shaking down in a new and changed environment. It was especially so during the winter of 1947. This was particularly severe and what made it worse there was an acute coal shortage. At one stage we had no coal except a heap of dust, and we were forced to improvise. We bought some cement and welded the small coal into balls which we burned as soon as the cement dried. They used to do this in Pembrokeshire using clay instead of cement. We survived with little illness among the children until the cold weather was over. Susan, our youngest, was born before the severe weather started. Then came a difficult time when all the children, except the baby, appeared to be constantly ill. It became increasingly pressing that somehow or other we would have to make a complete break. Florence had struggled during the war years and was at the end of her tether. I was trying to do an unsuitable job I should never have gone back to. I should have heeded the advice to change it, but at that time it was more easily said than done. Florence, during the time I was away, had been doing some spells of teaching at a local school, and she had taken classes of teenage girls in the evenings whenever she had someone to mind the children. She got great relief from these classes after being housebound for so long.

After worrying over our position for weeks, and after a series of illnesses that were a warning that the family—all of us—would quickly go downhill if we went on as we were, a way presented itself. Florence, instead of going her usual way doing her shopping, took a different route. She passed a newspaper shop where a copy of an education journal was displayed on a rack outside. She bought the journal and took it home. That was the beginning of a slow but certain movement that took us out of the slough that we had been in since the war ended. There was the headship of a school going in Suffolk. It was in a village called Blaxhall, close to Snape, the site some years later of the Aldeburgh Festival concert hall. Florence was interested in the area because her great-grandfather had come from near Woodbridge which she had visited as a child. She decided to apply as there was a house attached to the school; and getting the job would mean that our main difficulty of somewhere to live would be solved. At the interview she liked what she saw of the village and the school that had thirty-six pupils, although she had some misgivings. The isolation of the village was probably the chief one: it was three miles from the nearest railway station, and there was one bus a week to Ipswich, the nearest large town. The village, too, had no piped water or electricity: lighting in the house and the school was by oil lamp and water was from a sixty-foot well at the corner of the playground. The rector, who was the chairman of the school managers, offered her the post, and she accepted provisionally. We discussed this when she returned home. It would be a joint venture: she would be responsible for the school and I would help whenever necessary. I for my part undertook to look after the younger children until we could get some domestic help, and to fit in my writing as best I could. This for me was the only way out; and having a batch of stories accepted by the B.B.C. and the publication of my first book by Gwyn Jones's Penmark Press with a few encouraging notices made my decision to freelance slightly less mad than it appeared. Yet I had no illusions about what I was doing, just as Florence had none about taking a teaching post with four children—two under school age. But desperate situations, desperate remedies.

On the Saturday following the interview I travelled up to Blaxhall, walking the three miles from the railway station as Florence had done. No one was at home at the school house and I had a good look round the buildings and the garden. I was attracted to the area. Blaxhall was a scattered village with small brick houses, functional rather than picturesque. We decided to risk the drastic escape from our difficulties. I planned to retire from school teaching and to claim a small pension for the years I had already served. We had the prospect of living in a house of our own, and Florence had release from the domestic claustrophobia she had suffered for four and a half years. Looking back on our last-ditch escape to Blaxhall, we saw it as a watershed in our lives—parents and children. The way ahead was still far from clear but we now felt unencumbered and were going forward on a sure course that was right for a family that had recently been delivered from a devastating experience.

We moved from London a few weeks before the autumn term began. Yet the cycle of the children's illnesses did not finish when we left: we had to leave Mary behind in hospital. Florence's mother brought her to Blaxhall a fortnight later. Before school started we had a chance to look around. After a few days, one of our difficulties solved itself. A young girl escorted by her aunt turned up from the next village and offered her services as domestic help. Mabel Sawyer stayed with us for three years. She got on well with the younger children, and she made possible the arrangement Florence and I had worked out: I kept the two younger children occupied during the morning, and either wrote or went into the school in the afternoon, and wrote again, whenever possible, in the evening. Florence's assistant, who was responsible for teaching the infants, came from the next village. Miss Packard was a gentle and conscientious teacher and together they worked as an efficient team. Florence was much happier now that she was exercising a skill that had been acquired over the years and had been bottled up for so long. Neither of us had an easy task at the beginning, yet we knew that to make the experiment successful would mean adapting to new circumstances and sometimes doing jobs that neither of us anticipated. For the first few months, it was 'make or break'. Neither of us had time to make friends in the neighbourhood and for months we saw no one except those who were directly connected with the school. Here Florence established herself from the beginning. Previously the school had followed the rural pattern in East Anglia of being an institution that had a conventional form in the minds of the villagers. The head teacher was considered as part of the 'establishment' that, it was soon clear, was still intact in this region. The teacher was on the 'other side' and parents visited the school only on rare occasions. Florence changed all that: she made the school more open and invited the parents to feel free to come whenever there was a legitimate reason.

I took time to settle down in my new role. But it was part of an inescapable bargain and I had to see it through. The two young children who were my charges in the morning were very good; and I had the advantage of coming from a very large family and I had experience with the very young that I hadn't suspected I possessed. I knew instinctively what to do in the little crises that often occur with small children. I attempted not too successfully to teach them to read but most of the time was spent in active pursuits—painting, cutting out patterns of paper, and going for walks. At the top of the lane that ran along the side of the house was Blaxhall Common, a hundred-acre piece of common land that was almost surrounded by the Forestry Commission's trees. It had been a tank training-ground during the war and it had been cut up, but it was quickly recovering. It had an abundant bird life, and there was hardly a square yard of the common that we did not explore during the eight years we lived in the village. We were on the common on most fine days, and I took the boys up from the school to play football once or twice a week on a patch of grass that was surrounded by the bracken and furze covering that took up most of the common land. One day, I remember, we got into trouble during our morning walk. I used to search for animals—ducks, geese, pigs and chickens—to amuse the two children. We saw some hens and we approached the owner who was feeding them in his 'yard' or allotment not far from his house. We had with us a young dog of the lurcher type that Matthew had acquired. There had been a heavy frost the night before and the grass was still white. As we got near, the dog jumped up against the wire fence and scared the chickens. After the squawking and the fluttering of wings it was clear that one of the hens had hurt itself. The old man—I came to know him and his family quite well afterwards—looked at it and immediately pronounced his verdict: 'She's broke her leg; broke her leg. It's the frost I reckon.' He said he'd have to kill the chicken; and later that day he brought it up to the house.

On the reading side, I became an expert in young children's literature: nursery rhymes, songs and all of Beatrix Potter's books. The copies of these books became battered and dogeared through constant use; but recently I came across an almost new copy of *The Tailor of Gloucester*. Evidently we had bought a new one, for it was a tale we had read over and over again. On the principle that it is a poor man who cannot capitalize on his own limitations I wrote some stories for the very young. These were chiefly centred on a white cat we had, called Candy, that had eyes of a different colour: one blue and one yellow. She was the 'pussy with the golden eye'. Some of these stories were broadcast, giving me the distinction of a series of scripts that ranged from the Third Programme to *Listen with Mother*.

I was in very bad heart for the first year or so we were at Blaxhall. The main trouble was isolation which was partially due to my loss of hearing, and to the remoteness of the village. Our only visitors were people connected with the school, and I myself had little contact even with these. For weeks on end I would see no one outside the family except tradesmen. Fortunately at that time there was a full complement of these: grocer, baker, butcher, and the oil man who weekly filled up our tank of paraffin. Jimmy Smy, the oil man, was also clerk of the parish council. He still had a horse and cart that carried a huge tank of paraffin and was festooned with household necessities. He was a very companionable man and I looked forward to a chat with him, my one link with the village until I got to know my nearest neighbours, Robert and Priscilla Savage. At first, approaches were made to get me involved in the village. People did not know that I had another job besides being husband to the schoolmistress, and I refused to take any office in the village's organization. I was anxious to prove myself in my new capacity of freelance writer. Most of my waking moments were taken up in thinking of writing plans to make money to contribute to the family kitty. In retrospect, I believe it would have been better if I had let things ride and taken a complete break from writing, just dealing with the calls that arose directly out of our situation: minding the children, occasional help in the school, the perpetual round of filling the oil lamps and their servicing, the drawing of water from the well. It had a pump, fortunately, but on the children's bath night it was a real chore: fetching the water, lighting the copper to heat it up and then pouring the used water on to the garden. Then in the spring there was the large garden to dig and plant. All this was enough to engage my full energy without plaguing myself with writing projects. But on thinking it over I suspect that all writing of any value arises out of stress such as this, when the body and the mind are more than fully engaged, and the normal consciousness is stretched and there is a stirring of the deeper levels.

But the main difficulty was that my self-esteem was involved: if I slacked off and did no writing I would not be earning any money. We were poor but not desperately so, especially as we had both been used to a more or less frugal upbringing and it was no real hardship for us to pinch and scrape. The first winter was difficult but infinitely better than the two winters we had spent in suburban London. So that in looking back it appears actually pleasant, especially the evenings in a warm living-room when the younger children were safely in bed and we relaxed in front of a large coal fire and the room was lighted by the soft glow of an Aladdin lamp.

In the spring there was an amusing incident that was a result of our continued isolation and the consequent shift in our values that were the outcome of the move. We had asked a friend to visit us from London. He was Jim Davies, a Pembrokeshire man. I met him at the school I taught at for a brief while on demobilization. He, too, had been in the R.A.F. as a member of a bomber crew. His plane had been shot down over Friesland, in Holland. He landed in a canal; got out and buried his parachute, and later contacted a small farmer who hid him until the Resistance arranged his escape. But he was caught and sent to a Stalag Luft. On the Allies' advance, the Germans sent the prisoners on the long 'death march' to the east. His visit to east Suffolk reminded him strongly of his stay in Friesland when he was concealed and befriended by the small farmer. The landscape, the climate and the brick cottages were the same; even the custom of hanging the harvested onions under the eaves of the roof, as I was already doing, copying the Suffolk practice to keep them through the winter.

Almost as soon as he arrived we introduced him to our local 'wonder'. During the previous summer housemartins had built a group of nests under the eaves of the school and the nests had survived a fairly mild winter unimpaired. When the martins returned at the beginning of May they expected to reoccupy them. In the meantime, however, sparrows had moved in and started to raise a family, or at least to lay their eggs. Now began a running battle, with the martins determined to evict the squatters and renew their occupation of their nests. The whole family had watched the battle that extended over a couple of days. The antics of the sparrows to slip back after they had been evicted, persisted: a sparrow would appear as if from nowhere as soon as one of the martins left the nest, being worried in turn by a pair of martins until the sparrows would finally have to concede possession. This, however, did not prevent them continuing their worrying tactics: feint dives in the region of the nest combined with a cacophony of aggressive chirping like hecklers at a political meeting. When we related the conflict to our friend Jim and had shown him the nest, his reaction was different from what we expected and very self-revealing to us. He looked with amazed wonder—not at the birds. How could the Evanses become so absorbed in such a trivial thing as battle among birds when only a few months before they were living in London, with all its attractions and, presumably, more understandable interests? We had already begun to shed the city's preoccupations. Had we known it, we had begun the slow process of reassessing our lives, giving them a new and surprising direction. And it was a stroke of luck that we did not recognize at the time that we had chosen to live in Blaxhall on the edge of an open heathland whose bracing and sometimes keen air restored us all to health. It was fitting that the 'temple-haunting martlet', a bird that carefully chooses the site of its nest, had confirmed our own choice by building its nest on the house in which we lived. It was a good omen.

During the first twelve or eighteen months of our arrival in Suffolk we were so preoccupied with the family and the school that we became very self-contained. I tended to avoid contacts that exposed my hearing difficulties. I sensed that this was bad and it underlay the depression that was a natural result of this withdrawal. Florence made contact with the Quakers at their meeting house a few miles away at Leiston, and she found it a refreshing break after a week at school: and I gradually came to realize that meeting people was the best kind of therapy and the best antidote to the reclusive life I was living.

It was a piece of good fortune that I had Robert Savage as my neighbour. He was a retired shepherd and spent a lot of time gardening and tending his pigs, which he kept in a yard opposite the school. They had a large family who had all left home except their eldest son, Willy, who was deaf and dumb. It was one of the children's delights to watch him or his father feeding the pigs. My contact with the Savages increased and I used to take my two charges to visit them when we were on our outings; they enjoyed watching the feeding of the ducks and the chickens. Robert Savage spoke a pure Suffolk dialect, and it was this that first alerted me to the historic wealth that was in this small village. He came from a long line of shepherds on his mother's as well as his father's side; and I recognized that many of the words he was using were centuries old, although most of them were obsolete in ordinary language. Many of them were technical words connected with the tending of sheep, and therefore had stayed alive; for the tending of sheep had not changed appreciably since the Middle Ages. Many of the words I knew through a reading of the sixteenth-century English poets, and I got a pleasurable shock through hearing them spoken by a man who took them for granted and used them as if they are a natural part of his heritage—as indeed they were.

He spoke of the time when he was a 'page' to a shepherd, and brought to light the medieval order where page was the first step in the hierarchy. He used the word 'tempest', the first time I had heard the word in ordinary conversation—apart from its use in poetry or hymns. It was in its old, particular usage of a violent thunderstorm. He said: 'There's a

tempest coming up the river'—the Alde estuary, hinting that an
electrical storm always follows the water. He used the word 'things' in its
old meaning of animals: 'Things hoolly like the grains from the
Maltings'. It was the rhythm and colour of the speech that I admired: 'I
went to feed the pigs, and there was a cloud no bigger than a load of hay
over towards Sherwood's. And I was a-coming back it just blacked out
and down it come. I was hoolly drenched!' or again: 'Willie now got the
gilt [a splayed sow] and it's a cosset [a young pig brought up by hand].
But it's settled down. Willie coached it and cosseted it, and he went and
lay down with it. And now's it's all right.' I once heard Mrs Savage
telling her husband when she found the cat had misbehaved itself:
'Throw the mucky owd cat abroad!' using the archaic meaning of the
phrase—out of doors. 'Squat' was another ancient word she was fond of
using: 'He knows it all, you may depend. But he's the one to keep it
squat,' that is, hidden or secret. Although he had been a shepherd for all
of his life there was no technical query about what happened on the
arable farm that he could not answer. He was my mentor as I was finding
my way about the dialect terms. I discovered later that most of the words
he told me were in Thomas Tusser's *Five Hundred Points of Good
Husbandry*. He knew them in what, I am sure, was their original
pronunciation; and he took me through the arable year and the niceties
of the fallows and the rotation of the crops, pointing out in connection
with the rotation that the shepherd had a good say in what crops the
farmer grew. The shepherd advised him what crops he would want for
his sheep and it would be a rash farmer who would ignore his shepherd's
counsel. One day he was describing to me a particular form of plough
share and I was making heavy weather of his explanation when he
said: 'Give me your notebook for a moment: I'll make a draught
[drawing] of it.'

# 14 · Robert Savage

About this time the Festival of Britain movement started and the Suffolk community council suggested that the villages should organize exhibitions of old rural and domestic objects that had gone out of use. It was dimly realized that the war had been a watershed and the pace of change would quicken up. Impressed by the potential of Blaxhall as an example of the changes that already happened, we decided to hold an exhibition in the school during the following spring. For this purpose we formed a committee. But the enthusiasm in rural East Anglia for a Festival was very lukewarm. It had been initiated by a Labour government and was therefore suspect, and at first none of the farmers in the village was interested. That we were incomers and had not been in the village long enough to start a village function was a natural reaction. But we pressed on after the education people and the school managers had approved of the project. Our committee consisted of a farm worker, Frank Shaw, as the chairman, two other farm workers, the milkman and a villager who worked in Snape Maltings. He designed the publicity posters and fitted up exhibition stands and so on. I myself volunteered to do the secretarial work. We split the village up between the committee members who volunteered to visit each house and ask the villagers if they had anything that would go into the exhibition. (We had already circulated them with examples of the kind of things we had in mind.) Each object would be insured and would be returned as soon as the days of display were over. We managed to get publicity for the event, notably through a London weekly journal who sent a photographer out to take some shots in the village. The exhibition was a success and was well attended by the schools and villages around. But more important than this was the impetus it gave to a reappraisal of the past by ordinary people, so that they began to dig down to their historical roots and to recognize that their memories of their forbears were valuable—indeed, more valuable than the objects that had been in the exhibition.

From what they revealed I was beginning to appreciate how deep these roots went. The dialect words, used unself-consciously by the people as an integral part of their environment, were as unremarkable to them as the tools they handled in the farm and the implements they used at home. These could all be referred to the historical layer from which they came. But many of the customs that came to light in the exciting upheaval caused by the exhibition in the uncovering of family memories, could not be related to any definite period. From an anthropological standpoint these irrational beliefs and customs were older than history itself; yet they were still cherished by the older people who were born in the last half of the nineteenth century and as valid, and to them as deserving of respect as the doctrines of the Church. The phrase 'the historic community' was to me a mere textbook definition before I came to Blaxhall: after my early years there it became a reality.

In early 1950 I acquired a hearing-aid. The National Health issued a model called the Medresco and I soon learned to use it. It literally changed my life. I was no longer an island in a crowd of people that could be reached only with difficulty, but almost a complete member of a group, participating in everything that went on. I could now sit on a committee with the assurance that I could get the drift of the business that was being discussed. Jimmy Smy the oil-man, who was also the parish clerk, now approached me to join the council. It was the beginning of a fairly long association. The position began to change, too, at home. Jane our eldest child had reached eleven and she was about to change schools. There was no child from the village attending a grammar school, and one of the reasons was its remoteness. A child would have to cycle five miles to the nearest market town and then catch a bus for a three miles' journey to Leiston. We decided to send Jane to the Quaker school at Saffron Walden. I justified this by my own experience of attending a grammar school in another town with the inevitable disadvantage of living in two communities. Jane got a scholarship from the local education committee, and by very careful budgeting we were able to send her brother and her two sisters to the same school. It was a good school and it was well worth our effort to send them there. But I was not able fully to justify choosing an independent grammar school with my political beliefs. Yet this solution was the only one possible in our case.

Except for the month preceding the exhibition my writing had gone ahead. I was now reviewing regularly for an educational weekly; I wrote a number of short stories for broadcasting and a children's serial for B.B.C. (Wales). I was also writing a novel about my home. Yet I found that my writing about Wales was getting less as I was becoming preoccupied with writing about Blaxhall. My natural and deepest allegiance was to my own country, and I felt resentment at being weaned from it. I then reasoned with myself: how could I continue to write about Wales when I had been away from it for so long? My writing about Wales was a product of the Twenties and Thirties; the country had changed during the intervening generation. On the other hand, I argued, James Joyce wrote about his early years in Ireland for the rest of his life, after leaving it as a young man. Yet Joyce's Ireland had been fleshed into him and he carried Ireland with him wherever he went. For me it was a real conflict, and writing about England was a kind of betrayal. It could not be resolved except perhaps by going back to Wales. And that, for obvious reasons, I could not do. Like all insoluble conflicts, I had to leave time to settle it. In the meantime my interest in Blaxhall and the Suffolk environment continued to deepen. Conversations with Robert and Priscilla Savage mellowed my understanding of the village; and I contrasted it with my knowledge of the hill farming community I had acquired during my boyhood and youth in south Wales.

Gradually I came to appreciate that the difference in the farming—pastoral in Wales and intensely arable here in East Anglia—was vital; and a study of arable farming was the bedrock of any understanding I would hope to acquire about this new environment. The difference extended well beyond the farming itself: it permeated the whole community and therefore helped to condition it. For arable farming demanded an almost military precision, a hierarchy in order to function properly, a closely knit organization, and this set a recognizable stamp upon it. One of the first marks I recognized was that it was not as free and easy as the pastoral community in Wales. There were more class nuances, more invisible barriers that someone from a different community would take time to appreciate. The East Anglian village was a tight community, and because of this there was infinitely greater caution in making judgements about other people, especially if they were people in authority. This was understandable, even as a legacy from the not-so-distant past when anyone who was outspoken in his observations about those in power in the community would soon find himself outside it. Another noticeable trait of East Anglian village life as opposed to Wales—at least the Wales that I knew fifty years ago—was the extreme reticence about certain topics connected with a close community. I suppose it is related to the caution already mentioned: people will not inquire directly for personal information but will wait and compile a mental dossier as information turns up. This compiling may take months. But the compiler takes great delight when it is finished. One of its exponents in a Suffolk village remarked after 'observing' for a long time to her own satisfaction: 'If you wait long enough in a village you'll know everything.' Here the reticence is not a measure of the lack of interest in your doings; it is simply that there exists a different technique of finding out. In the Wales of my youth, if you were visiting a different part you were likely to be asked, 'Where do you come from?' 'Where are you staying?' And even 'When are you likely to leave?' East Anglians, I quickly found out, dislike being asked a direct question. It may well be thought that these observations are well out of date considering the massive changes all parts of Britain have experienced during this century. Yet it is likely that they will be found to persist; for the way this basic pattern grows out of the method the community uses to get its living from the land, having taken thousands of years to develop, will hardly change in its essence over a hundred or so years. It cannot be so easily expunged.

As time went on I saw that Robert Savage's walks past the school to tend his pigs got less frequent. His rheumatism—the bane of the shepherd's old age—got more and more crippling. He spent most of the day in his old Windsor chair in the living-room. He sat there day after day while Priscilla did her chores. He had a thrush as a companion. It would light on a bush just by the window and call his attention by its singing. He got great delight from this bird, sometimes calling out to his wife in the kitchen: 'Can you hear ma lil' owd bud, Mother? He's a-going some fine this morning.' Latterly, one of the family had bought him a budgerigar and he had the cage not far from his chair; and he talked to the bird as though it was a member of the family. Our two young daughters had a good deal of enjoyment visiting Robert Savage, to hear the bird and watch its antics. We visited him on the last day he was alive. He had been off-colour all the week and he lay in his bed that had been brought downstairs in the room next to the living-room. I went in the room to have a word with him and then went to talk to his wife who was in the next room with the two girls. Presently his wife heard a movement and went to see whether he wanted anything. She called me immediately. Robert was having a heart attack. He had raised himself and sat on the edge of his bed, probably in an attempt to ease the pain. We laid him down; and it was all over in a few seconds. There was nothing we could do. The old lady was expecting it and was quite composed. I asked her whether I should call a neighbour who was often in demand on these occasions. She said: 'I'll not have anyone lay a hand upon him!' I told her I would ring Dr Keer, and I went back to the next room and sent the girls home telling them I would soon follow them. Mary, who was seven at the time, said to me with wide eyes as they left: 'The bird has stopped singing!'

I was pretty sure the doctor could do nothing but I rang to tell him that Robert Savage was very ill. He soon came over. He knew his heart condition and he could see what had happened. He was a family doctor of the old school, and knew Robert well and was visibly affected by his death.

After the doctor had gone, I asked a neighbour to telephone for Priscilla's youngest son, David, who worked on a farm a mile away. When I went back she had gone upstairs to get the things she had prepared for such an emergency. She was quite clear and direct: 'Nobody shall lay a hand on him,' she repeated. 'You and me can see to him together.' We soon laid him out. She instructed me, when I asked, that you should lay the hands by his sides so that he would lie quite naturally. He was still quite warm when we had finished and he looked very peaceful. Her son David arrived soon afterwards and I left. I was glad that chance had so ordered it that I should be there in her real need.

I was fond of Robert Savage, and would always be grateful to him for he was the first to communicate to me the feel of the old community of which he was a sterling member. He was my interpreter (although he was not aware of his function) of a large tract of history that for me before I met him had remained unquickened. He it was who gave me entry to what was a foreign country that, without his help, I would never have known. Later, after the funeral, Priscilla Savage told me that the thrush that sang outside the cottage went away after Robert's death: 'The day he died, it sang—oh it did sing; and he said to me: "Can you hear my babe?" I've heard that they even follow to the churchyard and sing there. Strange, isn't it?' I made no comment. If she believed that the bird was a fellow-mourner it would have been wrong to cast doubt on her conviction.

Needham Market

# 15 · A Village Play and a Film

As a result of my confidence in the hearing-aid I accepted the invitation to put up for a vacancy on the Blaxhall parish council. The parish council was a remnant of the old medieval parochial council, the body that used to be responsible to the village for electing its officers, the parish clerk, the constable, the overseer of the highways and the overseer of the poor. In its present form it was a new body dating from its formation in 1894. It was the weakest member of the chain of local government. Yet although it had only minimal powers, for instance the freedom to levy a small rate for improvement of parish amenities, it had great potential for complaint or agitation if improvements in the parish were slow in coming. There was plenty of room for improvement in Blaxhall. We had no water, no sewage system and no electric light, and a very inadequate public transport service.

Once elected I discovered that there was a National Association of Parish Councils organized in each county, each having sub-branches in their constituent district councils. The National Association could make representations direct to the government; and this was an extra means by which the parishes' interests could be promoted. After I served on Blaxhall parish council for a year Jimmy Smy, the clerk, resigned through age and I volunteered to take his place. As a member of the council I could receive no salary, but that did not worry me unduly for the reason that it would make my election virtually certain. I now felt that as clerk I could do something positive to get the much needed amenities for the village. I had a feeling that the village had accepted the position of being last in every queue. The people seemed reconciled to their position. In fact one of them told me that the reason for Blaxhall's neglect was that there were no 'big names' in the village. Although I was sure I would never be that, nor even the surrogate of a 'big name', I was convinced that if people were behind me, we could accomplish in time as much as any big name.

I was elected to represent the council on the district branch of the Parish Councils' Association. This meant attending meetings at Woodbridge, eight miles away. There was no transport and it meant cycling. I should say that this was not altogether a display of public spirit on my part: there was a great deal of private interest in it. Ever since we came to the area we were doubtful about the purity of the water that came from the school well that we were using. When we first came to the village, at frequent intervals we suffered as a family from stomach upsets. Most newcomers suffered in the same way. A cynic was of the opinion that you would suffer until you became 'manured' to it. Florence on inquiry found out that there was a local belief that the school well 'wasn't a good one', and for that reason no water was served with the school dinners. Eventually we had the water in the school well analysed. This showed that the bacteriological findings were satisfactory; but the chemical content of the water was not investigated. Reports in the press had told us that very young babies developed cyanosis through being given well water in their food, and some had died. The offending chemicals were nitrates which were poured in tons on the soil of this intensely arable area as farm fertilizers.

Once we knew the real problem I made up my mind to do all I could to urge the district council to hurry the scheme to bring piped water to our village. I made myself an aggressive nuisance in meetings and in letters to the press. I also wrote to our local M.P. who took up the question with the Minister of Health. The position was that the membership of the local district and county councils in East Suffolk after the war had no real urge, no motivation to improve the general conditions in the parishes. It was a perfect example of what was in essence class government, however unconscious. Members of the rural councils were people of one class—people who could afford to give up one or two days a week to attend meetings in the town and who were able to run a car to take them there. Thirty years ago this meant they were 'moneyed' people—'independent people', the Suffolk natives called them. They

included retired military men, ministers of religion, retired civil
servants, well-to-do farmers. Only rarely was a member without a
substantial income a member of a district or county council. The only
two I knew at the time in East Suffolk were men who were employed in
the town in firms like I.C.I., and were allowed time off to attend
meetings. There was also a man who was a small farmer, who had once
been a miner in Derbyshire. The result was that although the majority of
members lived in the country, they were isolated from the disadvantages
that country living involved; for they had provided for themselves the
amenities of electric light and piped water. A farmer, for instance, was
able to bore an artesian well from which he pumped water by means of a
petrol engine; and by the same means he could generate his own
electricity. They were nearly all landowners or comfortable tenant
farmers on large estates, and human nature being what it was, they were
not very enthusiastic about schemes that would involve an increase in
the rates levied by the county and district councils. Most of them, while
formally agreeing that the country, on humanitarian grounds, should
have the same basic amenities as the town, were not pricked with the
same urgency to bring this state about as those who suffered from their
absence.

The campaign to get piped water in the villages gained some impetus
from the death of another young baby in the county from well-cyanosis.
This was not caused, as already suggested, by bacterial infection and it
was not prevented by boiling the water that the baby drank. It was due to
the presence of nitrates that came from the shallow wells: the nitrates
were reduced to nitrites and this had caused the trouble. Before taking
this up with the local M.P., I took the precaution of reading some of the
medical literature about cyanosis in journals like the *Lancet*. I also went
to London to the library of the American Embassy in Grosvenor
Square. Well-cyanosis was first detected in America and there was a
great deal of relevant literature there to support our case.

I do not know what effect all this activity had on the eventual arrival of
piped water in our village. I suspect very little, but at least it did not deter
it. Yet the Blaxhall parish council certainly speeded up the arrival of
electricity. Most of the villages near us had had electricity for some time
but we were without it, and with little prospect of getting it. Accordingly,
in the parish council we decided to by-pass all local government
organizations and appeal direct to the Minister of Housing and Local
Government. At the time he was Harold Macmillan and our appeal to
him had a certain piquancy. His wife was a sister to Lady Blanche

Cobbold who lived at Glemham Hall in the next parish and was Lord of the Manor of Blaxhall, and theoretically responsible for Blaxhall Common. Both sisters were daughters of the Duke of Devonshire. We drafted a letter to the minister and appended to it the signature of every householder in the parish. Just before it was sent a member of the district council unsuccessfully tried to stop it. The letter and the signatures were posted. The poles went up round the village and light came shortly afterwards. A comment from County Hall was typically double-edged: 'The crying baby gets the milk!'

Our son Matthew had recently joined his sister at Saffron Walden, and only the younger girls were at home during term-time. We still used to wander about the heathland after afternoon school had finished. In the autumn we picked acorns to sell to the Forestry Commission; in the spring we looked for nests and observed the birds. It was my ambition to hear the cuckoo again, as I had not heard it for years. Both the girls had very sharp hearing, like their mother, and were able to pinpoint the spot where a bird was calling. I remember on one walk, not far from Blaxhall church, following them as they tracked a cuckoo that was calling and then kept moving. They were as pleased as I was when it stopped on a tree and I heard it quite plainly. Afterwards, they improved on this occasion in a mischief-ful way. Mary would wander off casually, and presently Susan would say: 'I believe I can hear the cuckoo.' I would then identify the note of a rather inexpert bird. After a while Mary would emerge from behind the trees: 'Did you hear it?' 'Yes, yes, perfectly.' They were much amused by their joke, and thought to repeat it until it became like the real 'cuckoo in June—heard, not regarded'.

In the spring we often cycled to Iken Cliff that was usually deserted at that time of year. We spent a long time watching the shelduck that nested there every year and lit up the drab scene with vivid flashes of colour. Later when they had hatched their brood, we watched them escorting their young in staid order around the inlets. One afternoon we were making for the beach and surprised a young seal that was sunbathing. We did not get near enough to him to examine him very closely. He soon slid away and hid himself in the muddy water. Another of our afternoon diversions at Iken Cliff was to search the bank of an inlet for Roman shards. There was a cache of them that would become exposed after the successive tides.

There was one particular amenity lacking in the village: it had no playing field. I had discovered the lack when I took Florence's boys from the school to play a game of football. We had to use an improvised pitch on Blaxhall Heath. Through the parish council, it was decided to buy a field adjoining the parish hall or 'room' as the Blaxhall people called it, a modest building that had been built on the corner of a field of a few acres. It could easily contain a football pitch and possibly a tennis court or two. In a corner it had a worked-out marl-pit that was part of the property. Buying the playing field was a major undertaking for a small village. Yet the people were very spirited and rallied together to organize various projects to raise the money. One of the most successful efforts was the adapting of the marl-pit to stage an open-air play. It required little shaping, simply the cutting down of the vegetation with which it was overgrown and a levelling of its floor for an auditorium. On one side there was a mound of earth that was covered with grass. It formed a perfect, natural stage. By the side of this the shrubs had been left to form a 'green room' where the actors could wait to go on to the stage. A very good amateur company from Ipswich volunteered to come out and give a performance. The play chose itself: *A Midsummer Night's Dream*. We got an extension from the mains of the newly won electricity and we borrowed floodlights. The evening was a fine one in June and the play was an outstanding success. Most of the older villagers had never seen a full-length play before, certainly not by Shakespeare, and they enjoyed the novelty enormously. They identified with 'the hempen homespuns' especially as they spoke in broad Suffolk. The high spot for the Blaxhall part of the audience was the first appearance of the 'translated' Bottom. One of them called out: 'My heart alive! Here comes Darcher's dicky.' Darcher Poacher was the man who formerly carted marl from the pit with his cart and his dicky was the donkey.

This was a very active time but I did not let these activities interfere with my writing. One of my projects was a pastiche of Spenser's *The Shepheards Calendar*. I admired this poem especially now that Robert Savage had initiated me into the shepherd's life and had virtually recapitulated the medieval shepherd's calling, for it had remained substantially the same up to the time he was a page. He used the same words as Spenser and Tusser and the same methods of tending and doctoring his sheep as they were doing in the poet's time.

During this year I met a remarkable woman, Mary Field, who was head of a film company producing children's films. In the constant search to increase my earnings I had submitted to her the synopsis of a children's story that I judged had visual possibilities. During my wanderings with the two girls I had come across an old mound in

Tunstall forest. It was obviously a burial mound, probably of the Sutton Hoo period. It was quite near Blaxhall Heath, not far from Snape, and completely surrounded by trees. Mary Field liked the idea of the film that was about three or four children who foiled a gang who planned to dig into the mound and rob the grave. She commissioned me to write the treatment for the film. The film was called *The Ship in the Forest* and was made in the area where the story was set. It had its first showing in the Aldeburgh cinema and we managed to get all the children in Blaxhall School, along with the Tunstall children, over to see it. I very much enjoyed working with Mary Field who was a master of her craft of film-making. In an hour or so's conversation with her, I learned more about films than I could have learned in a lifetime of film watching and reading about them. She had thought deeply about films, and her Carnegie Report on children's films illustrates the thoroughness of her methods.

This report revolutionized the making of children's films. It arose out of her observation that it was possible to gauge a group of children's reactions to a film simply by watching their actual physical responses. Restlessness and constant shifting of their position on the seats were obvious signs that their interest was not fully engaged, while a marked increase in the number of children leaving to go to the lavatory was a devastating criticism of the film itself. The technique she used in compiling her Carnegie Report was merely an extension of her commonsense observations. She did her studies in Saturday morning matinées, filming the children's full physical reactions while the film was being shown. She used infra-red film that made filming possible in the dark. She was able therefore to study a film she had made, scientfically matching the children's facial expressions and movements with the relevant passages of the film.

She had also made a study of various dramatists to improve her approach to film-making, and she recognized that her main problem was identical with that of the early dramatists, who had a milling crowd before or around the action on the stage, as much bent on having a holiday as on seeing a play. The playwright had to capture the composite audience of the pit right at the beginning with an arresting first scene, as Shakespeare did in *Macbeth, Romeo and Juliet, The Taming of the Shrew*, and some of the historical plays. He knew that he had to win over the groundlings or else the players would have difficulties. We had a perfect example of this in the London première of the Suffolk film. It was held in the King's Road, Chelsea, in a huge cinema at a Saturday morning matinée. I took Florence and our four children to see it. We were given seats in the upstairs circle, and below us was a real 'pit' audience of turbulent young Cockneys. They were supposed to be watching the climax of an American film that was supporting the Mary Field film; but most of them were doing everything but watching the screen; they were writhing about, and from above it looked like a free-for-all encounter rather than an audience. The film's action had been designed as an exciting climax: the rescue of the heroine, an attractive, barely clad young girl who had been tied by the villains to a post in a rapidly burning building. Most of the children, however, were unconcerned and the noise was uproarious. We wondered how they would ever be able to show the Suffolk film in this bear garden. Yet as soon as the first shots were shown on the screen the children were captured. It was a pure triumph by a master of children's film-making. The opening shots were of a couple of children—a boy and a girl—and an old man, as far as I remember, an old fisherman. Immediately the audience identified with the children, and strangely enough, with the old man: the film had their full interest instantly and retained it until the end. It was one of Mary Field's discoveries that young children are not interested in middle-aged adults but are naturally interested in children of their own age on whom they can easily project their own feelings; also in people who are old enough to be their grandparents.

I was also connected with Mary Field in another way. She was a history graduate and first entered the film industry by making documentary films for showing in schools and colleges. She joined Gaumont British Instructional Films in the early Thirties; and she made a series of documentary films in East Suffolk, not far from where we were living in Blaxhall. She had the brilliant idea of filming the arable farming as it was in the mid-Thirties. She set out to make a record of current practices in farming, but being a perceptive historian she knew that some of the methods still being used then had a very old provenance and she sensed that, with the advent of the tractor, farming was changing rapidly. One particular farming process was the thorough- or under-draining of the land—bush-draining, so called from the use of hawthorn bushes in the narrow draining channels. This was a technique that was at least as old as the coming of the Romans to Britain. The series of films she made in Suffolk fifty years ago are now valuable historical documents; and interest in them has been revived through the work being done by the Audio-Visual Centre at the University of East Anglia in Norwich. I owe a particular debt to Mary Field because her films were part of the impetus that urged me to write my first two East Anglian books that are chiefly about the old farming in Suffolk.

Mary, our third child, was now due to leave Blaxhall School and go to the Friends' School in Saffron Walden to join her brother and sister. We decided to move. As we did not run a car our isolation became more pressing: if Florence could get a school near a main railway line it would mean that the constant journeys into Essex would be much easier. A school was going in Needham Market, which had a station on the Cambridge line, a bigger school, and she got the appointment. We were lucky enough to be able to rent a big period house that few people seemed to want. It was a very old property, an open hall house as it was discovered later. The huge attic had been unoccupied for years but it was probably used as a work place and store by an early owner in this fairly prosperous wool-combing area. I became interested in the surface details of the house which I wrote about later. Susan, who was then about ten years of age, had very sharp eyes and spotted many construction marks and merchant-marks on the timbers and doors. I measured the dimensions of the ground floor, made a plan of the house on squared paper, consulted local documents, and gathered all the information I could from local people. But I had already started on another Suffolk book, the second, and could not spend much time yet on a fresh subject. Two or three months after we left Blaxhall in 1956, Faber published *Ask the Fellows Who Cut the Hay*, and I was surprised at the reviews it got. I was much encouraged though sales were very modest at first, before the mass interest in country books and local studies had really got under way.

We lived for six years in Needham Market and we contrasted it with the fruitful, hard but enjoyable time we spent at Blaxhall. Needham was once a market town but had lost much of its status to nearby Stowmarket, which had grown in importance. In spite of its being the administrative centre for the district of Gipping, it had the atmosphere of a town that had seen better days. The market which had once been held in the wide main street had long ceased; and its local reputation rested mainly on the holding of a lively carnival during the summer to raise funds for local causes. Part of our rather jaundiced view of Needham was caused by our own difficulties. Florence now had a bigger school with a staff of half a dozen or so. The school was not in a good state when she took over and it took some time to settle down. I was left more to myself and was able to do more work. Although the house was structurally absorbing, I found the darkened beams and other timbers, especially the panelling in two of the rooms, and the successive alterations that excluded the light, very oppressive. And with only Susan at home the house was as quiet as the tomb.

One of our friends at Needham Market was the vicar, Hargrave Thomas. He was the son of a Birmingham Welshman. He had graduated at Lampeter, the Welsh college that had its charter early in the nineteenth century. The college trained, almost exclusively, priests for the Church. Hargrave Thomas was High Church and I equated him with Conrad Noel of Thaxted, though he was not as well known. He was a socialist and a county councillor and very outspoken. Shortly after his first coming to Needham Market, there occurred the General Strike of 1926, followed by the lock-out of the miners. He spoke at an open-air meeting in Ipswich in support of the miners. It was a brave thing to do and the result was immediate: he lost a great deal of his congregation to a neighbouring church. For years his congregation was depleted by his championing of the miners; and he must have been affected by the exodus. But he did not show it; and continued there until his retirement in the late Sixties.

Our house stood opposite the church and he used to call in quite often. He was a school manager and Florence saw a lot of him as he took his duties very seriously. One of my first impressions of him was his walking down the street. He was wearing his black, wide-brimmed 'Devil-Dodger' hat (the Needham people called it his 'Sandeman's Port' hat) and his long black cloak. When I looked closer I could see two pairs of little shoes coming towards me each side of a pair of heavy hobnailed boots in the centre, processing in two rhythms which somehow were accommodated to one another. When he got nearer he opened up the cloak and two little boys he had enfolded on their way to school darted out merrily, laughing at their game with the vicar. He had a mischievous streak in him that delighted in puncturing any aggresive pomp or ceremony. On one occasion he had to appear at the magistrate's court in Ipswich to speak a few extenuating words on behalf of a village youth who had kicked over the traces. It was his custom to carry a bag of peppermint sweets in his pocket and he would offer them to anybody—usually at a well calculated moment. The real reason for his carrying peppermints, however, was to console an old horse that spent a lot of its time languishing in a field near his home. On the occasion of his visit to the court, he took out his peppermints and proceeded to hand them round to those people within reach, a studied plan that only fell short of his handing them to the magistrates on the bench. This was a wily ploy to defuse the carefully induced atmosphere of the court and attempt to make it more relaxed.

I myself was a victim of one of his more unusual performances. One Christmas-time he had arranged a service of Nine Lessons at the church, to be celebrated on a Sunday afternoon. Just when we were about to sit down to our midday meal Hargrave Thomas called. He was in great difficulty. He could not raise his full team to read all the lessons. He was two short: 'Will you and Matthew help an old priest? You can read the Priest's Lesson!' I demurred and told him that he did not want his service to be compromised by an old pagan like me. But he persisted, and to humour him Matthew and I attended the service. Yet it did not end with the reading itself. He had fixed up Stations of the Cross and finally he had us all processing down the church, some of us bearing objects like statuettes and crosses. We met at the centre aisle and finished up at the altar. I responded to the old boy's enthusiasm and so did Matthew; but for years afterwards we had to suffer ragging from the rest of the family who reminded us of our appearance in the Needham procession.

As a family we did not fit in with the community as we had done at Blaxhall. This was chiefly because the children spent most of their time away, although they took part in social events when they were home, and Matthew played for the town cricket team. But part of our unease was due to Needham's having all the disadvantages of a town with few of its benefits. We lived on the main street, a busy road that took all the traffic from the coast to the Midlands. Another factor was that our children had reached the stressful time of adolescence. Our two older children had a comparatively easy transition, but the whole pattern of society had seemed to change by the time Mary, our third child, changed schools when we came to Needham in 1956. A new post-war generation was percolating into the schools and it showed itself most vividly in the children who were just starting on the secondary stage of their education. They were more sophisticated, had grown up more quickly, and were readier to question what adults expected to be unquestioned. As far as we were concerned as parents, the most important value they questioned was the authority of adults. We could see it not only in our own family but in the schools; and it was a hard lesson to learn that the child was entitled to his own view and did not have to defer entirely to his elders. We had to adjust, as we were bound to acknowledge the adolescent's right to do so. It was like going through a course for re-educating parents: we gradually recognized that we had been brought up under an authoritarian system. We had been brought up to give unquestioning obedience to parents and to the school authority. You listened to the master and you rarely questioned him; and in university the lecturers and the professors breathed a different air. The professor was as remote as a little god; you could rarely get near him. Brett, the English professor at my old college, was the 'sport' who proved the rule that professors were distant and hedged round with an impenetrable air of authority. This was especially true in the newer universities where the ratio of staff to students was not as generous as in the older universities, where the tutorial system operated and where contact in a residential college was much closer between all members of the university. I recognized that the new 'revolt' of the young was a much needed and healthy departure as long as it did not proceed too far and promote a counter-reaction.

This is a post-crisis judgement. It was not so easy to be rational and understanding when you were in the middle of it and had the Old Adam sitting on your back: 'This is the behaviour parents used to expect from their children: they used to treat them with respect! How will they finish up if we allow them to get away with this or that?' On looking back, the main trouble arose from the confrontation between an old accepted attitude lasting into a post-war revolution where social values were in a flux and the family was adrift in the middle of it. The young after the mid-Fifties appeared to think like this: 'We are told to listen to our parents, to obey and to respect them. But how can we respect them if they are not *respectable*?' The young had moved with the times while their parents in their eyes were standing still, wrestling with social customs and observances that were long outmoded. Adolescence is a turbulent time: I remember my own and I do not admire it as I look back and imagine my parents' part in it. They did not insist on categorical imperatives: they were temperate in their demands and their expectations. This, in the memory, was a great governor of our own conduct when our children were finding their feet. We could still give advice but we had to take their reaction in a process that was not one-sided, in the sense that the parents were being initiated into a new life as much as the children. At this point, families confront the rapids, and depending either on luck or skilled piloting they emerge into the smooth water at the other side. Many family boats are upset. We ended up, *laus Deo*, on an even keel, and remain a close family without estrangement twenty years later.

Helmingham

# 16 · *Extramural Work and Radio*

On Hargrave Thomas's recommendation, I became a member of Needham Market parish council. But after my hyper-activity at our previous village, I took my membership more tepidly. My only excursion to the County Hall to an annual parish councils' meeting was to air a local grievance and to make a plea for a public lavatory. Our living in the main street gave us ample opportunity to observe how visitors found it difficult to satisfy their bodily needs. We both now felt we should like to move back into the country. Florence wanted a change, and a country school a few miles away with a rather large attached school house presented itself. The school was at Helmingham, the ancient seat of the Tollemache family who built the school at the same time as they remodelled the village in the middle of the nineteenth century. It was opened as a boarding school for farmers' sons and a day school for children of the adjoining villages. In its early years the school was attended by the Tollemache boys. The only class distinction appears to have been that the boarders had a separate entrance. A few years later, a boys' boarding school was opened at nearby Framlingham and it gradually creamed off the Helmingham boarders and the school became an ordinary village school. The school house was unusually large for it contained the dormitories of the boarders as well as accommodation for the headmaster and his family. John Tollemache who built the school, incorporating features of the Tudor Helmingham Hall in its design, also built model cottages with Tudor, high-pitched roofs, each pair of cottages standing in an acre of ground. A nineteenth-century Ipswich radical praised John Tollemache for his treatment of his workers and for his public spirit, and compared him with the other Suffolk landowners who failed to win his plaudits. He appears to have been a benevolent aristocrat who expected, in spite of his progressiveness, or because of it, to be given as of right absolute control of the village. His aim seems to have been to construct an ideal little commonwealth of landowner and workers. One of the tenants of the 'double-dwellers', the semi-detached cottages, told me that John Tollemache wanted only two sorts of people in the parishes where he owned nearly all the land: the rich and the poor. He didn't want any in between. His view was of a bi-polar society that excluded the middle class. He was going back in history to the period before the emergence of the middle class—the capitalist class; but it evidently worked on the scale that he had built the estate and he proceeded to run it himself.

The Hall with its moat and drawbridge was in a park where some of the oaks that Constable painted still stood; and while we were there in the Sixties men from the estate kept the roadside trees in perfect order. It was a great lift to us to live again in the country in a well kept environment in a quiet village with a windmill on a hill in sight of the school, instead of on a main road where the bedroom windows had to be permanently shut to keep out the exhaust fumes of the traffic. It was a two-teacher school and Florence had an excellent assistant; and I was at hand in an emergency, to take the boys for football or for a swimming lesson. Most of our cares seemed to lift once we had settled in Helmingham and the children were more content, each having a bedroom of their own. Susan who had in time gone to the same school as her brother and sisters had not settled, and now lived at home, travelling daily to the local grammar school. Shortly after we got to Helmingham we were able to buy a car and this made it possible for me to do more B.B.C. work and to lecture regularly with the Cambridge University Board of Extra-Mural Studies and the Workers' Education Association. Although it was not economic for a freelance writer to do this work, I enjoyed it very much as I was able to discuss with some of the members sections of a book I was writing on the folk life of East Anglia. Many of the members of these classes were graduates and we had some interesting discussions during the lectures. I met some good people, and by keeping to my current interests, which formally were politically neutral, I avoided controversy and kept as objective as I could.

There was a cross-section of people attending the classes but they were chiefly middle class. Yet one member stays in my memory as a man who came up with stimulating and fresh ideas. I enjoyed having Horace White in my class. He had had little formal education but he was an example of a man whose education had begun in war. At the end of the First World War he met a fellow soldier, an Australian, who stimulated him to think for himself. When he returned from abroad he refused to take farm work. The wages were then twenty-five shillings a week. He worked on contract as a hedger and ditcher, and on any job that he would be paid with an agreed wage. When I first met him he worked for the drainage board as a regular employee. By then he had become a parish and district councillor. He served on the district council with Adrian Bell, the Suffolk writer, who was friendly with him. He was respected in the councils and in W.E.A. classes for the freshness of his views and the way he defended them. Before the First War and during it he had a very rough time; yet it did not make him bitter. His opinions and beliefs arose out of his own experiences, discussed and sharpened by debate in the councils and the adult classes. He was not a great reader of books, though he was a memory storehouse of all the people he had met and of all the experiences he had gone through, all conveyed in a completely individual form of address that was smoothed by his patent sincerity. His thinking was his own and it was plain when he took part in a discussion. His views rode over the simple and often improvised language he used to express them and were fresh and compelling. I was impressed by him as a man who, in spite of what some people would call lack of polish, had something to say and invariably said it convincingly.

Another man I recall as being a stimulating member of the adult classes was the rector of Boxford in Suffolk. The Reverend Pearce-Higgins had been at universities in Britain and the U.S.A. but had not let higher education dessicate his humanity. He was the very opposite to Horry White but both had that quality that encouraged any teacher to whom they were exposed to dig down further and uncover their best. The B.B.C. area station at Norwich was opened in 1956 and although I had already given short talks from Broadcasting House before this, it was through David Bryson, who was the first head of the Norwich station, that I had a chance to take part in a series called (ironically for me) *Through East Anglian Eyes*. Through him I also borrowed a B.B.C. portable recording unit to record some of the older Blaxhall people before we left the village. It was the first B.B.C. portable recording machine and it was called a 'Midget'. As one of the men I recorded said to me: 'If that's a Midget how big are the grown-up ones?' It was a battery-operated machine, heavy to cart about, especially with a separate pack holding the microphone and the tapes. Yet it was a very good machine. I still hold the eight five-inch tapes I made at Blaxhall twenty-seven years ago, in good condition in spite of their losing some of the higher frequencies, probably through not being stored in archive conditions. But it was not until I could manage to run a car when we came to Helmingham that I was able to do the kind of radio programme that I had in mind. The use of the portable unit at Blaxhall had shown the possibilities of making programmes out of 'actuality' recordings in the setting of a linking narration, such as the features made on the Third Programme by writers like the Irish poet W. R. Rodgers—particularly his own programme on James Joyce.

Since working on my first Suffolk book I had developed the technique of interviewing farmers and farm workers, and I became more and more convinced that what they were telling me was valuable historical data. They were coming to the end of a period of farm history that had had a comparatively uninterrupted course since history began. The internal combustion engine had effectively broken that continuity, as indeed the introduction of the steam-engine to ploughing had done, in a formal sense, in the previous century. Yet the steam-engine was unsuitable owing to the haphazard shapes of the field: its weight, too, was injurious to the soil. The latter doubt was particularly active among farm horsemen when the tractor was first introduced. When they worked with horses they would not allow a horse so much as to put a hoof on land that had already been ploughed. The old horsemen when I recorded them at the end of their long careers had a concern for the soil that almost amounted to veneration. It was a kind of animism. It was Horry White who once said in a class discussion: 'The soil is just. Treat the soil well and it will yield of its best.' Many of the old farmers, too, had reservations about the compaction of the soil by the big machines. But the machines rode on and changed the face of the countryside, and what is even more important, changed rural society irrevocably. I felt it especially important to record the feelings of farm people about the new era that was just beginning, for the reason that they were living through the greatest revolution in farming since Neolithic times. As well as recording their thoughts about the new farming, it was my idea to make a record of the era that had already vanished, if only to demonstrate the massive continuity that inhered in so many practices and customs linked with the tradition of hand tool farming that was now disappearing.

Another reason, apart from the purely historical one, for my continuing to record the old people was the valuable linguistic evidence that I was gaining. I had started with the Blaxhall people and it was evident from the 'prentice' recordings I had obtained in that village that a rich store of language could be collected in this way. The language they used was beautiful and arresting, and the history that was hidden in the words themselves was worth the closest attention. As I have already written, it was the splendour of the language often spoken by the old people that first attracted me and induced me to examine the whole community where it was richest—those people who had been tied to the soil and had the centuries-old tradition in its most rewarding form. How much more valuable would be a record of the language on magnetic tape that would give an exact reproduction and would skip the laborious exercise of transferring speech into phonetic script. My experience in the R.A.F. gave me confidence that I could handle a recording apparatus expertly enough to get a good result; and David Bryson's arranging for a B.B.C. engineer to bring me a recording unit and instruct me in its use ensured that my first recordings would be technically up to standard.

At this point I made contact with David Thomson, a producer of country programmes associated with Laurence Gilliam who was himself largely responsible for the Third Programme. He came up to Helmingham and together we visited and recorded a farmer and an old horseman in that area. He stayed a night or two and left me to get additional material from old horsemen I had got to know in the weeks that followed. I was impressed by David Thomson. He had an unusual background, and valuable experience that admirably fitted him to edit such a programme as we were proposing. After finishing university he had gone to southern Ireland coaching the children of an Anglo-Irish family, as he has recorded in his book *Woodbrook*. He finished up virtually managing the estate farm. Therefore he had a unique experience of country life and he also had the sensitivity to absorb its less obvious nuances. We were also in complete accord in our estimate of the countryman, the so-called unlettered countryman who had been comparatively untouched by the commercialism that was quickly sterilizing country life. We both reacted to him in exactly the same way, finding him deeper in many ways and more rewarding as a subject than those who self-consciously paraded their letters and posed as his betters.

Therefore, when David Thomson proposed a programme about the Suffolk arable farm, the subject of farm horsemen chose itself. In the book published a couple of years before, I had begun my study of farm horsemen; and I had collected a great deal of additional information from farmers and horsemen all over Britain. They had been stimulated to write about some of the material I had included in the book. One fascinating letter came from north-east Scotland. It was from Norman Halkett, a farmer's son from Aberdeenshire but who was now living in Thurso not far from John O'Groats. He is a man about my own age who is passionately interested in the farm horse. He was particularly keen to learn about the inner ring of East Anglian horsemen who had the secrets of the drawing oils and jading substances, and especially in those men who had practised the ritual of the frog's or toad's bone. In a series of letters he explained that he was a member of the secret Society of the Horseman's Word; and without breaking the oath to the society, that he undertook to keep on entry to it, he told me a little about its organization. I became very involved in this material for the reason that I recognized from his description certain features proving conclusively that at bottom it contained evidence that it was very ancient indeed. In the first place, it came from the same cultural level as the society of Freemasons, which essentially stems from pre-Christian cults. The Roman Catholic Church, with its acute nose for heresy, very early recognized this and as a result still refuses to acknowledge the Freemasons even today.

David arranged for me to visit Norman Halkett in Thurso, and I flew up and recorded him. It was a quick but very enjoyable visit in the early part of the year; and the recordings very effectively rounded off the programme. It went out a few weeks afterwards and was well received. It was the first of many programmes I did with David Thomson. The glimpse of the ancient historical layer I had obtained in researching into the lore of the farm horse convinced me that the social anthropologists would have had a fine harvest of material in Britain if instead of going out *en masse* into the colonies and the rest of the world, some of them had stayed at home and studied the communities in the rural areas of Britain and Ireland. And if from the data they had already gathered from these undeveloped societies abroad, and in the light of this, they had gone back to the rural pockets at home that had been comparatively untouched by the twentieth century, they would have gathered a haul that would have surprised them. John Layard, an Oxford anthropologist, did research before the First World War in the islands of Malekula Vao in the Pacific New Hebrides. He found that the natives still celebrated rituals that were linked with the Old Stone Age level of their society. They were of a pattern just referred to in connection with the Scottish Society of the Horseman's Word. They were, too, the basis of the corpus of rites that the Freemasons, at the beginning of the eighteenth century, adapted to form the basis of their speculative society. A Roman Catholic priest was on the islands at the same time as Layard and his colleagues. He recognized the primitives' ritual as a 'mystery' in the same sense as his Church uses the word. This, with its similarity to the Masonic rites, inhibited him from writing anything about it. Survivals such as this would confirm the findings that, as some archaeologists such as Colin Renfrew point out, join the earliest reaches of the past with the near-present.

A few of us spent a great deal of time in the mid-Sixties in an attempt to form a rural or folk life museum in East Anglia. It was proposed that this would house the remnants of the society that was quickly passing away: the farm tools and rudimentary machines, and the visible evidence of the material culture and especially the rich oral information from the last generation of people who had used the tools, and so on, and had lived most of their lives within the climate of the old farming. The idea had the support of the local authority and we looked for a big house with extensive grounds that would give room to develop a museum on Continental lines. I very much admired the Welsh Folk Museum that Iorwerth Peate had pioneered at St Fagan's near Cardiff just after the last war and hoped that it would be possible to found a centre in East Anglia on similar lines. The University of East Anglia at Norwich was in the process of foundation and although it had no students yet, we approached the vice-chancellor with the suggestion that they should include within the university a museum or centre that would be a focus for the study of the region, and develop into a centre for encouraging the collection of such related disciplines as folk life or social anthropology and the dialect. In the event, two factors told against the idea: the University was more concerned to establish a School of English and American studies; and again, although we speak of East Anglia as though it is an entity, it has little regional consciousness. In a cultural sense it is only a name, although a recognizable geographical entity. The idea eventually foundered on an intense county chauvinism; and separate establishments were set up in Suffolk and Norfolk. The project failed, and I had the late intuition that we were attempting the impossible. There was no group consciousness—even minimally disseminated—that could encourage us to believe that the unit of East Anglia, except as a loose term of reference for a physical region, was a viable historical concept. Looked at realistically it was one of history's hazier fictions. Even the University of East Anglia, which later set up a centre of East Anglian Studies, appears to have been threatened recently, in 1982, by the new god of Economy. So during the latter part of our stay in Helmingham I returned to my cobbler's last and began to hammer out a new project.

The children grew up quickly once we had left Needham Market. Jane had moved to Camberwell to study art, and shortly afterwards Matthew had entered the London School of Economics. For the greater part of his school life he coasted along, enjoying school with his chief interests in football and especially cricket. In later years at school he was inspired to work, and after passing his first examination he decided to specialize in economics and studied it during his last two years. Mary, who I always thought had ability as a writer, decided to teach and went for training at Homerton, Cambridge. Susan, after she left the grammar school, went to Dartington to study drama. We found Helmingham very pleasant to live in. Everything was neat and well cared for. It was the mark of a 'close' village that, if one was prepared to accept unreservedly the authority of the landowner, life could be very tolerable. If you could not, the ultimate sanction would be applied and you had to move out. We were fortunate in our position. The school and the school house, though owned by the estate, were on a long lease to the county education committee and we were not under the aegis of the resident lord. But Lord and Lady Tollemache called on us to welcome us to the village and were very friendly. Lord Tollemache was a member of the military side of the family and had little experience of managing a country estate; and that was soon noticed by the older tenant farmers on his land. There was not the apparently instinctive understanding of their problems that they expected from the landowner. Yet the position was complicated by the quickly changing conditions in farming. By the mid-Sixties the landowners were beginning to find that it was more profitable to take the farms into their estates and farm them themselves or through an agent. One of the Helmingham farms was so managed while we were there. A farmer, who did not have a son to succeed him, retired and the estate ran his farm while the house was let to a retired military man.

Lady Tollemache was very good-hearted and did a great deal for the village, especially for the school children and the old people. At Christmas, the school children were invited to a party at the Hall. Lady Tollemache carried out the preliminaries punctiliously. Each child received a personally addressed invitation. She told Florence that she logged all the functions she was responsible for in a big notebook, so that as they recurred each year she could consult it and go through the event without a hitch. I attended the party on one occasion and the entry in the notebook must have been something like this: 'Transport, time of arrival; children to the lavatory; butler to announce each child by name; games [listed] in the medieval hall; tea in the big dining-room; Lord T. to supervise the pulling of the crackers after tea (must be simultaneous); lavatory again; film-show in library, Mickey Mouse etc. Climax; back to the medieval hall to the presents on the Christmas tree. After; Lord T. looks at his watch: "Silence! I hear a bell. [Bell off stage] Hark! I hear Father Christmas! He's coming over the drawbridge in his sleigh." Enter Mr Mitchell [the chauffeur] dressed as Father Christmas. (Every night he drew up the drawbridge which he had just crossed.) Lady T. welcomes Father Christmas and helps him give out the presents. After some of the excitement subsides, Lord T. looks at his watch again and says: "Six o'clock!" and with precise military dismissal, "Time to go home. Goodnight."'

Only once did Florence see a sign of the iron hand in the Tollemache velvet glove. The county council had a new policy of supplying identification boards to their schools. A board was erected in resplendent new paint outside Helmingham School, complete with the coat-of-arms of the East Suffolk County Council at its top. The arms were the rub. The first time Lord Tollemache saw it, he was almost apoplectic with annoyance. No other coat-of-arms should be displayed on his estate. Who was responsible for it? Florence received him calmly and explained that the officials of the county council had erected it on all their schools as a routine exercise. All the while Lady Tollemache stood behind him as though to cool him down. But his bad humour soon vanished and relations with the Hall were invariably friendly until we left. Yet when we first came to the village I was a bit nervous about how I would shake down in such an environment. All my beliefs were against the exercise of hereditary privilege, and my natural impulse was not to disguise my reaction to it. I was, however, in a sensitive situation, and a parade of my true feelings would embarrass Florence's position. I would have to appear as merely the headmistress's husband, as a cypher on the school house backcloth. In my contact with the Tollemaches, little as it was, I became much more tolerant than I had once been. My former attitude was that the rural structure of lord or squire and the community that those titles presupposed was long out of date and the hereditary peerage was an anachronism. I often examined my changed stance while we were at Helmingham. Maybe I was getting more release through my partial fulfilment as a writer and from the enjoyment I was getting from the adult education work. The lessening frustration through worrying about my low income was also a factor that made me less taut. Or perhaps, now that I was older, a kind of biological conservatism had set in and had slowed down my physical rhythm, and with this slowing down had expunged some of my prickly insistence that a better all-round standard of social life could be attained and should be consistently aimed at. For there was a danger of becoming a superannuated 'yes-sayer' and a mere boring praiser of past time. Yet I had still sufficient belief in my own integrity: I was convinced I had something to say and in my more sanguine moments I thought that it was valuable, and that my main intent should be to say it.

I found myself taking less part in village affairs. Owning a car gave us more freedom of movement, and we took advantage of it. We began to widen our activities, to see friends more frequently and visit places we had little chance of seeing before. Ease of movement became very necessary but you have to pay a price for owning a car—in more senses than one. The car can be a great dissipater of local interest. In our first Suffolk village of Blaxhall, the only transport we had as a family was cycles, and this alone was largely responsible for helping to nurse our growing interest in the community. We did not use the village simply as a dormitory: we got to know the people well, lived close to them and to a great extent shared their hopes and their disappointments. I am sure that living day after day with our neighbours and identifying with them was the fullest and most satisfactory episode of our period in East Anglia. We became identified with the people of Blaxhall in a way that lasted. After our children were married, one of the first visits they made was to Blaxhall to show their spouses where they had been brought up, looking on the village as almost solely the focus of their childhood memories. Not always were visitors enlightened at their first sight of the scattered village: a small church standing away from the nearest houses; no distinctive or picturesque cottages, only modest and unpretentious brick-built dwellings that were not even very old. I have often heard it said by people who are seeing it for the first time that there is little to distinguish it as a village. I always counter by saying that it is the people that give a village its character and stability and not the buildings. It is they who transmit its qualities and give it its imprint. These are not uncovered by a cursory visit but only by living among the people and discovering their virtues. Although these are not paraded, they are the real and abiding element of the village's individuality.

We were coming to the end of our stay in Helmingham. The family was paired off and either married or about to be married, and Florence was about to retire. We had been looking for a house for some months, and our first thought was to go back to the Cambridge district that we had been visiting increasingly of late as Mary was at college there. We played with the idea of getting a house in the centre of the town. Jane, our eldest daughter, had married a Fellow of one of the colleges and they were likely to return from U.S.A. where they were living temporarily. We had a house surveyed off Trumpington Street in Cambridge but the report was indifferent and we were dissuaded from making a bid for it. This was the fortunate outcome of a sentimental wish to return to the Cambridge of the Thirties. We should never have settled down in the different environment of a university town after living for so long in villages. We were thus saved from the results of a costly mistake. We next looked about in Suffolk, but without success. Then a friend told us he knew of a cottage just over the Norfolk border where he lived. Eventually we bought a small thatched cottage there. We estimated that we had enough money to restore it, and Florence gave in her notice. We moved into Norfolk in 1968, and our twenty-year stay in Suffolk came to an end.

In approaching the close of this truncated account of my life—a kind of interim report on an unfinished journey—there is a temptation to make a partial estimate, ignoring any *respice finem* doubts and pausing for a moment to take breath, looking back on the ground already covered and paying little regard to the unseen country over the hill. It has not been a particularly eventful journey in terms of adventures recorded or countries visited, but it has been lively enough, at least in the mind that is not anchored to the body or confined to home-keeping habits acquired partly through inclination and necessity. It is hard to decide whether the journey followed the dictate of chance or whether it grew out of the nature of the traveller, who consequently fitted or deserved it. Yet one fact is certain: some of us are well equipped from the start to go on a journey of any kind; some are not so. Yet they make a creditable progress on it by a little spark of determination or inspiration that transcends the limitations they are born with. I count myself lucky to be born when and where I was and have never wished to have grown up in a different setting, human or topographical. A child can make a heaven of where he finds himself even though it seems to the world an unfavoured place. As long as the human environment is stable all is well: that is the only setting that really touches him. The rest is incidental. The valley where I grew up was sometimes grim but the hills beckoned to a larger country that held the story of centuries of my people that has become the lengthy prelude to my minuscule experience. In estimating the various incidents in its text I find that there are passages that I wish to forget, yet it is from these that I got experiences that were valuable. These were the times that were not easy to live through but which brought what little wisdom I have: a conviction that while you savour your successes you learn from your failures: it is through them that you temper your mettle. Achievements tend to diminish with time, even through your own eyes; for your values change and your former pride in them loses some of its lustre. Your reverses, however, leave a more lasting mark. They are the scars that you attained in an honourable battle and will reassure you in any conflict still to come.

In writing down my own story I was reminded of our custom of reading stories to our children when they were very young. I remember our three-year-old son on one occasion telling me his preference for a certain kind of story: 'Read me', he said, 'not one of those stories out of a book but a story out of your tummy.' I have taken the hint here and have followed the implied advice that the solar plexus rather than the head is the seat of all true and individual story-telling.